Praise for The Blended Workbook

"Blended learning is the rocket fuel for innovation in education. Through this practical guide, Horn and Staker step readers through powerful examples and probing questions which unlock the promise of using technology to transform learning."

—Richard Culatta, CEO, International Society for Technology in Education (ISTE)

"*Blended* is a guiding light for the teachers and leaders we support, but implementation is tough and the road is long, so practical workbooks like this are essential tools for ongoing efforts to personalize learning in schools."

—Shawn Rubin, chief executive officer, Highlander Institute

"Michael Horn and Heather Staker have written an excellent follow-up to *Blended*. If you need a framework that inspires superintendents and principals to transform education, start by reading their work. It is the best blend of vision, theory, and practical ideas available in our field."

—Cary Matsuoka, superintendent, Santa Barbara Unified School District, Santa Barbara, California; board member, The Learning Accelerator

"Understanding the theory about blended and its variations is a basic requirement. For successful, sustained implementations of blended learning, it's key to develop thorough understanding and skills in this arena. If you are serious about education for *all* students, then *The Blended Workbook* is essential reading and practice."

—Dr. Kenneth W. Eastwood, superintendent, Middletown City School District, New York

"*The Blended Workbook* is a definitive guide for school districts and teachers ready to jump from 'personalized learning' as a buzzword to transforming the educational experience for students. The video links and scenarios provide rigorous opportunities for a team to dive deep into understanding the components of blended learning and the steps for effective implementation."

—Dr. Lisa Garcia, superintendent, Point Isabel ISD, Port Isabel, Texas

THE blended WORKBOOK

Learning to Design the Schools of Our Future

Michael B. Horn ▲ Heather Staker

JOSSEY-BASS™
A Wiley Brand

Published by Jossey-Bass

A Wiley Brand

One Montgomery Street, Suite 1000, San Francisco, CA 94104-4594—www.josseybass.com

Jossey-Bass books and products are available through most bookstores. To contact Jossey-Bass directly call our Customer Care Department within the U.S. at 800-956-7739, outside the U.S. at 317-572-3986, or fax 317-572-4002.

Wiley publishes in a variety of print and electronic formats and by print-on-demand. Some material included with standard print versions of this book may not be included in e-books or in print-on-demand. For more information about Wiley products, visit www.wiley.com.

ISBN 9781119388074 (paper)
ISBN 9781119403586 (ebk)
ISBN 9781119403548 (ebk)

Cover design by Wiley
Cover image: © hakkiarslan | Thinkstock

Printed in the United States of America

FIRST EDITION

PB Printing 10 9 8 7 6 5 4 3 2 1

Contents

Acknowledgments

This book would not have been possible without the generous assistance of many educators in Texas who allowed us to use their blended-learning plans to provide the critical examples that make this book come to life. In particular, thank you to the following schools, school systems, and educators who are doing all they can to help every student they serve succeed:

- Austin Achieve Public School's Emily Morrison, Development Director; John Armbrust, Founder and Executive Director; Joe Ten Brook, Vice Principal; Greta Kwedar, Vice Principal; Julia Barraford-Temel, Computer Science Teacher;
- Birdville Independent School District's Randy Sumrall, Senior Project Leader; Cheryl McKnight, Project Manager;
- Cisco Independent School District's Amy Dodson, LRC/ Blended Learning Director; Kelly West, Superintendent;
- Clear Creek Independent School District;
- Georgetown Independent School District's Alma Guzman, Executive Director of Professional and Digital Learning; Kim Garcia, Director of Digital Learning;
- Grand Prairie Independent School District's Sharon Thornton; Jennifer Oliver; Maury Ayres; Elizabeth Hart;
- KIPP Houston Public Schools;
- Leander Independent School District's Wendy Jones, Director of Instruction, Learning, and Innovation;
- Mineola Independent School District's Kim Tunnell;
- Pasadena Independent School District's Dr. Karen Hickman, Deputy Superintendent of Academic Achievement; Vickie Vallet-McWilliams, Director of Instructional Technology; Jeanne "Nina" Conway, Executive Director of Business Services; Toni Lopez, Executive Director of Curriculum; Stacey Barber, Principal; Roneka Lee, Principal; Steve Fleming,

Principal; Catherine Birch, Teacher; Stefanie Cantin, Teacher; Lori Deardorff, Instructional Coach;

- Point Isabel Independent School District;
- Round Rock Independent School District's Dr. Patricia Ephlin, Principal, Robertson Elementary; Dr. Amy Grosso, Grants Coordinator;
- Spring Branch Independent School District's Julie Hodson, Director of Grants;
- Temple Independent School District's Luann Hughes, Director of Technology; Jason Mayo, Principal; Lisa Adams, Executive Director of Secondary Education; Jacki Wright and Jessica Mays, Instructional Technology Specialists;
- Tulia Independent School District's Daniel Keith, Director of Instructional Design;
- Ysleta Independent School District's David Medina, Principal at Pasodale Elementary; Norma Corral, Principal at Ysleta Elementary; Kathleen Mendoza, Campus Technologist, Pasodale Elementary; Maria Rivas, Campus Technologist, Ysleta Elementary; Micha Villareal, Innovative Learning Director; Brenda Chacon, Associate Superintendent.

In addition, Pamela Barrier has provided critical on-the-ground support to help Texas educators in crafting and implementing their blended-learning plans, as well as advised us with this book.

We also thank our colleagues from the Clayton Christensen Institute for Disruptive Innovation, where this work began for both of us. In particular, Julia Freeland Fisher, Thomas Arnett, Clifford Maxwell, Ann Christensen, Hayden Hill, Katherine Mackey, and, of course, Clayton Christensen, remain wonderful colleagues and inspirations to us.

Our agents, Danny Stern, Kristen Karp, and Whitney Jennings of Stern Strategy Group, remain valuable supports for our work. We owe a debt of gratitude to Kate Gagnon, our editor, Cathy Mallon, and the rest of the editorial team at Wiley who helped bring this project to fruition. Anne Hoffman, senior director of curriculum and assistant professor of practice at the

Relay Graduate School of Education, also helped us improve the rubrics used throughout the book. Anthony Kim, Mike Wolking, and Janice Flynn Vargo from Education Elements also contributed valuable insights.

Finally, this project would not have been completed without the support of two critical members of our team. Heather's development associate at Ready to Blend, Theresa Carter, stepped in time and again to provide research support. And Nancy Messegee contributed heroic efforts on tight timelines to help us identify and fine-tune the blended-learning examples and explanations that appear throughout the book. We could not have done this book without her.

About the Authors

Michael Horn is the co-founder of and a distinguished fellow at the Clayton Christensen Institute for Disruptive Innovation, a nonprofit think tank. The chief strategy officer for Entangled Ventures, an education technology studio, and a principal consultant for Entangled Solutions, which offers innovation services to education institutions, Horn speaks and writes about the future of education and works with a portfolio of education organizations to improve the life of each and every student. He is the coauthor of the award-winning book *Disrupting Class: How Disruptive Innovation Will Change the Way the World Learns.* Visit him at www.michaelbhorn.com.

Heather Staker is founder and president of Ready to Blend, a training and consulting firm that provides keynotes, workshops, and multiday deep-dive professional-development programs that help school leaders and teachers use blended learning to improve the achievement and well-being of K–12 children. She is also the co-founder of Brain Chase Productions, an online program that challenges students to learn in the context of a larger adventure story involving real buried treasure. Prior to these roles, she was a senior research fellow at the Clayton Christensen Institute for Disruptive Innovation. Visit her at www.readytoblend.com and www.brainchase.com.

THE blended WORKBOOK

Introduction

This workbook is for all educators—teachers, teachers-in-training, school leaders and administrators, and parents—who are involved in designing learning environments in schools and want something more for students. It will help you get the most out of our book *Blended: Using Disruptive Innovation to Improve Schools.*

In this book, we walk you and your team step-by-step through exercises that mirror the design process in *Blended.* Most of these exercises were developed and refined in workshops that we, along with our colleagues at the Clayton Christensen Institute, have given over the last several years to help educators design and implement blended-learning environments. The origins of several of these exercises lie in the work of our friends at Innosight, a consulting firm that Clayton Christensen cofounded, before we adapted them to an education context. We are grateful for their foundational work in helping organizations innovate.

Throughout the book, we not only provide concrete exercises for you to work through in designing a blended-learning model but also provide sample answers from real schools that have designed blended-learning environments. These examples serve as tangible models for you to reflect on, see what is possible, and build your capacity to design and evaluate. Many of these examples—good, bad, and mixed—have been culled from real answers to these very exercises by teams in school districts that designed their own blended-learning models in workshops facilitated by Ready to Blend, which Heather Staker founded.

This book is organized sequentially. It starts with helping you understand the basics of blended learning and assess whether you're ready to get started. Then it helps you mobilize to bring together a team around a purpose for blending. Next, it walks you through a design process that builds on itself, by starting with helping you design the ideal student experience, then the ideal teacher experience, then the ideal physical and virtual environment, and then finally bringing it together in a coherent set of instructional models. The book concludes with implementing: helping you establish a winning culture up front, prepare a budget, and mitigate the risks as you innovate.

Even though the sequence builds on itself, you can dive into any part of the book that would be useful to you. If, for example, you already understand the basics of blended learning and which models are disruptive to a traditional classroom, then skip Part 1 and start with the module where you need support. If you are doing blended learning already, focus on the modules that will help you improve what you have in place. Just as learning should be personalized to maximize student success, it should be personalized to maximize your success as well.

Whenever possible, we recommend using this guide with a team of your fellow educators to maximize your vision and impact across a school or district.

It's time to design the future.

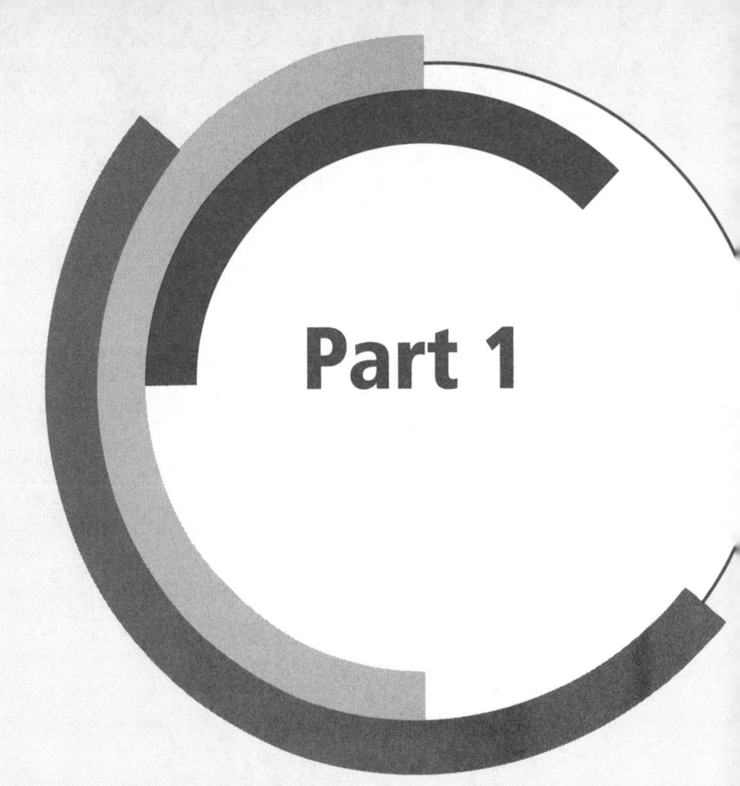

Understanding the Basics and Getting Ready

The Basics of Blended Learning

Key objectives

- **Identify what is and is not blended learning**
- **Recognize and distinguish the models of blended learning**
- **Predict the types of circumstances where each model works best**

Content summary

Overview of blended learning

The future of education

Today's students are entering a world in which they need a student-centered schooling system. Student-centered learning—the opposite of what we call today's predominant factory-model school system in which students learn in lockstep—is essentially the combination of two related ideas: personalizing learning and competency-based learning (also called mastery-based learning, mastery learning, proficiency-based learning, or sometimes standards-based learning).

Personalizing learning

There are several notions of what personalized learning is, but when we say it, we think of it as a verb: personalizing learning. That means tailoring learning to an individual student's particular needs—in other words, customizing or individualizing to help each individual succeed, given that students learn at different paces, possess different background knowledge, and harbor different interests that ignite their learning. The power of personalizing learning, understood in this way, is intuitive. Research shows that when students receive one-on-one help from a tutor instead of mass-group instruction, they typically do significantly better. This makes sense, given that tutors can do everything from adjusting their pace if they are going too fast or too slow to rephrasing an explanation or providing a new example or approach to make a topic come to life for a student. A personalized approach also implies that students can receive a one-on-one learning experience when they need it, but can also partake in group projects and activities when that would be best for their learning.

Competency-based learning

The second critical element of student-centered learning is competency-based learning; that is, the idea that students must demonstrate mastery of a given subject—including the possession, application, or creation of knowledge, a skill, or a disposition—before moving on to the next one. Students don't move on from a concept based on the average pace of the class or within a preset, fixed amount of time, as they do in the traditional factory-model school system. Competency-based learning embeds aspects of perseverance and grit because in order to progress, students have to work at problems until they succeed; they can't just wait it out until the unit is over. If students move on to a concept without fully understanding a previous one, it creates holes in their learning. No wonder Sal Khan and many other luminaries have latched on to the many studies that show competency-based learning producing better results than time-based learning.

Blended learning as the enabler

When implemented well and jointly, personalizing learning with competency-based learning form the basis of a student-centered learning system. An important part of student-centered learning is that students build agency so that they can ultimately be effective lifelong learners, which is necessary in today's rapidly changing world, in which knowledge and skills become outdated quickly.

The challenge lies in how to implement student-centered learning at scale. Paying for a private tutor for every student would of course be wonderful, but it's prohibitively expensive. Differentiating instruction for each child—a step toward personalizing learning that teachers across America try valiantly to do—is difficult in today's factory-model education system. Similarly, allowing all students to progress in their learning as they master material may be possible in a school with a small student-to-teacher ratio and flexible groupings, but it is taxing on an individual teacher who has to provide new learning experiences for students who move beyond the scope of a course, and it therefore strains the resources of most schools.

This is why blended learning is so important. Blended learning is the engine that can power personalization and competency-based learning. Just as technology enables mass customization in so many sectors to meet the diverse needs of so many people, online learning can allow students to learn any time, in any place, on any path, and at any pace—at scale. At its most basic level, it lets students fast-forward if they have already mastered a concept, pause if they need to digest something, or rewind and slow something down if they need to review. It provides a simple way for students to take different paths toward a common destination. It can free up teachers to become learning designers, mentors, facilitators, tutors, evaluators, and counselors to reach each student in ways never before possible.

Of course, just because a school adopts online learning does not guarantee that learning will be personalized or competency based; we wrote *Blended* and this accompanying workbook to help educators and students around the world realize these benefits. The blend of online learning into schools marks the most powerful opportunity the world has known to make student-centered learning a widespread reality.

What is blended learning?

Blended learning is critically different from—but easily confused with—the much broader trend of equipping classrooms with devices and software. The common use of "blended learning" in education circles and the media suffers from a Goldilocks problem. People use the term either too broadly, to refer to all education technology ("edtech") crammed into a classroom, or too narrowly, to point to only the types of blended learning that they like best.

Beginning in 2010, we interviewed the educators behind more than 150 blended-learning programs to arrive at a "just right" middle-ground definition that is broad enough to allow for variation but narrow enough to differentiate it from the bottomless category of edtech in schools. The definition has three parts.

Blended learning is:

- Any formal education program in which a student learns at least in part through online learning, with some element of student control over time, place, path, and/or pace;
- The student learns at least in part in a supervised brick-and-mortar location away from home;
- The modalities along each student's learning path within a course or subject are connected to provide an integrated learning experience.

One note for clarity. When we say "modalities," we mean the different mediums and formats in which a student learns—whether the learning occurs online, offline, in a project, through direct instruction, and so forth.

Blended examples

Blended provides a breakdown of each of these parts of the definition. This section offers hypothetical situations to help you understand whether a student is experiencing blended learning.

Scenario 1

Dominique's teacher posted all of his lesson plans, assignments, and quizzes on Blackboard's learning management system. Dominique can access this class page online from her brick-and-mortar classroom or from home using the tablet her school loaned her.

This is not blended learning. Because the Internet is only hosting information and tools for Dominique's class, but is not managing the delivery of content and instruction—the face-to-face teacher is doing that—Dominique does not have control over the time, place, path, or pace of her learning. The class is learning the same thing at the same time and moving through the curriculum as a single batch, or perhaps in a few groups, instead of using an online platform to serve each student the right level of content at each moment of learning. Dominique is in a "technology-rich" classroom, but not a blended one.

Scenario 2

Matthew is a full-time student at Mountain Heights Academy. He completes his work on his own off campus but connects with his online teachers live via webcam and Skype video-conferencing software. He also uses Skype to connect synchronously with the school's virtual chess club and virtual student government.

This is not blended learning. Matthew is not learning in a supervised brick-and-mortar location away from home. He is a full-time virtual school student, not a blended learner.

Scenario 3

Twenty students in a class are working on Khan Academy at their individual, appropriate level. Meanwhile, the teacher is working with ten other students who are all struggling with the same concept.

This is blended learning. Because students are learning at their own pace and the online and offline learning are connected—that is, the teacher is using the online activity to inform how to target instruction and what students do offline—it is blended learning.

Check for understanding

Is it blended?

Here are some opportunities for you to practice identifying whether a student is experiencing blended learning. The answers and explanations are in an appendix at the end of this module.

1. A teacher assigns students a group project in which they use Google Docs to collaborate on the writing and research.

   Blended learning? Yes No

   Why?

   ____

   ____

2. A teacher shows an online video in class during a lecture to help illustrate a point.

   Blended learning? Yes No

   Why?

   ____

   ____

3. Students choose from a list of learning resources that include videos, texts, and simulations to master content so that they can pass a quiz testing their knowledge of tectonic plates.

   Blended learning? Yes No

   Why?

   ____

   ____

4. Students play Minecraft after completing their regularly scheduled class work in geometry.

   Blended learning? Yes No

   Why?

   ____

   ____

5. Students use a math program that provides practice problems with varying difficulty based on the questions they answer correctly and incorrectly. Meanwhile, the teacher uses this data to track the progress of the class.

   Blended learning? Yes No

   Why?

   ____

   ____

6. Students work independently through an online course as a teacher periodically calls them into one-on-one meetings to discuss their progress.

   Blended learning? Yes No

   Why?

   ____

   ____

Content summary

Models of blended learning

Blended learning generally looks different across different classrooms and schools, but typically fits somewhere within the broad parameters of four main models.

Rotation model

This category includes any course or subject in which students rotate on a fixed schedule or at the teacher's discretion between learning modalities, at least one of which is online learning. Other modalities might include such activities as small-group or full-class instruction, group projects, individual tutoring, and pencil-and-paper assignments. Students learn mostly on the brick-and-mortar campus, except for any homework assignments. Broadly speaking, there are four different types of Rotation models:

1. Station Rotation—a course or subject in which students experience the Rotation model within a contained classroom or group of classrooms. The Station Rotation model differs from the Individual Rotation model because students rotate through all of the stations, not only those on their custom schedules.
2. Lab Rotation—a course or subject in which students rotate to a computer lab for the online-learning station.
3. Flipped Classroom—a course or subject in which students participate in online learning off-site in place of traditional homework and then attend the brick-and-mortar school for face-to-face, teacher-guided practice or projects. The primary delivery of content and instruction is online, which differentiates a Flipped Classroom from a class in which students are merely doing homework practice online at night.
4. Individual Rotation—a course or subject in which each student has an individualized playlist and does not necessarily rotate to each available station or modality. An algorithm or teacher sets individual student schedules. An individualized

playlist is a curated set of online and offline resources, lessons, and activities through which students learn. In some cases, students have a prescribed pathway; in others, students have the choice of how to navigate the playlist.

Flex model

This category refers to a course or subject in which online learning is the backbone of student learning, even if it directs students to offline activities at times. Students move on an individually customized, fluid schedule among learning modalities. The teacher of record is on-site, and students learn mostly on the brick-and-mortar campus, except for any homework assignments. The teacher of record or other adults provide face-to-face support on a flexible and adaptive as-needed basis through such activities as small-group instruction, group projects, and individual tutoring. Some implementations have substantial face-to-face support, whereas others have minimal support. For example, some Flex models may have face-to-face certified teachers who supplement the online learning on a daily basis, whereas others may provide little face-to-face enrichment. Still others may have different staffing combinations. These variations are useful modifiers to describe a particular Flex model.

A La Carte model

This model encompasses any course that a student takes entirely online to accompany other experiences that the student is having at a brick-and-mortar school or learning center. The teacher of record for the A La Carte course is the online teacher. Students may take the A La Carte course either on the brick-and-mortar campus or off-site. This differs from full-time online learning because it is not a whole-school experience. Students take some courses A La Carte and others face-to-face at a brick-and-mortar campus.

Enriched Virtual model

This category includes any course or subject in which students have required face-to-face learning sessions with their teacher of record and then are free to complete their remaining coursework remote from the face-to-face teacher. Online learning is the backbone of student learning when the students are located remotely. The same person generally serves as both the online and face-to-face teacher. Many Enriched Virtual programs began as full-time online schools and then developed blended programs to provide students with brick-and-mortar school experiences. The Enriched Virtual model differs from the Flipped Classroom because in Enriched Virtual programs, students seldom meet face-to-face with their teachers every weekday. It differs from a fully online course because face-to-face learning sessions are more than optional office hours or social events; they are required.

Figure 1.1 offers a diagram of the terms. In many cases, schools use multiple models and combine them in different ways to create a custom program. The purpose of these terms is to provide a shared language to describe the basic building blocks of the various combinations.

Figure 1.1: Blended Learning Models

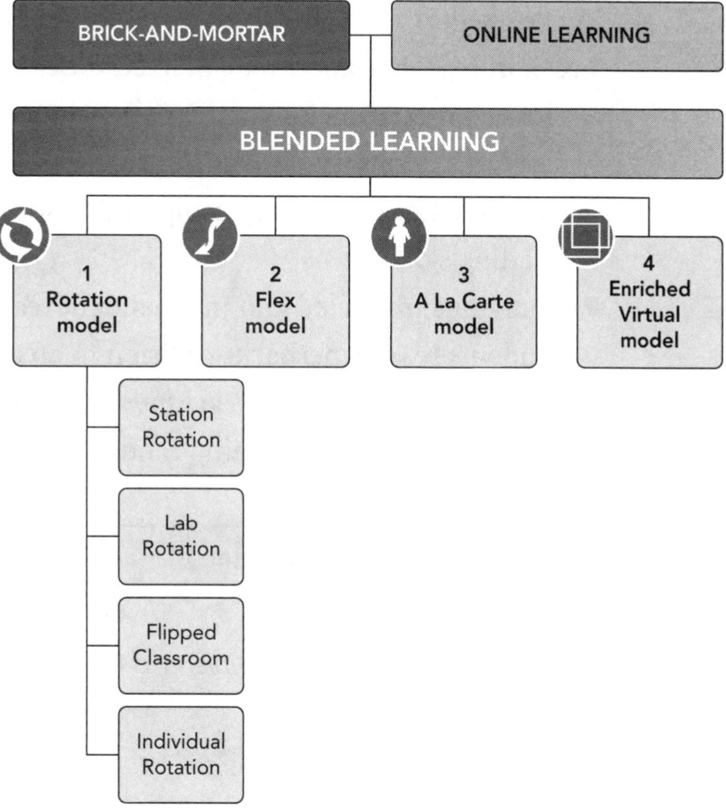

Understanding and using the vocabulary of the blended-learning models serves two purposes. First, it helps you communicate your vision to other stakeholders. When you explain that your design involves a Flipped Classroom combined with a Flex model, for example, other people with at least a basic familiarity with blended learning get a preliminary idea of your intentions in only a few words. Second, naming the models helps with your research and development. Other blended programs across the world are tagging their designs with the names of the models. Enter the model name in an online search at the Blended Learning Universe or in Google, for example, and you will find examples of other blended programs that resemble your design.

Blended model examples

This section provides hypothetical situations to help you identify the different models of blended learning.

Scenario 1

A class begins with a whole-group discussion. Students then break into groups and rotate at fixed times through three stations:

- Small-group direct instruction, in which the teacher uses resource books and works closely with individual students
- Individualized learning, using online software to practice reading skills
- Individual modeled and independent reading, in which students read paperbacks or listen to an audio book

This is the Station Rotation model. Students are rotating on a fixed schedule among learning modalities.

WATCH CLIP 4: Aspire ERES Academy uses a Station Rotation to facilitate differentiated instruction.

www.wiley.com/go/blended4

Scenario 2

Students rotate between traditional classroom learning and a computer lab for their online learning, where they learn at their own pace.

This is the Lab Rotation model. Students are rotating on a fixed schedule and go to a lab for online learning.

WATCH CLIP 7: Rocketship Education relies on a strong culture and an innovative staffing model to facilitate its Lab Rotation.

www.wiley.com/go/blended7

Scenario 3

Students watch Khan Academy videos online at home and then come to school, where they engage in practice and projects with their fellow students and the teacher.

This is the Flipped Classroom model. Students are learning online from Khan Academy at home in place of doing traditional homework and then attend the brick-and-mortar school for face-to-face, teacher-guided practice and projects.

WATCH CLIP 9: Some teachers at DongPyeong Middle School flipped their classrooms to engage their students and boost learning.

www.wiley.com/go/blended9

Scenario 4

All students rotate once in their math class, but while one child learns online by himself for both rotations, another child works in a small group with the teacher and then in a group project for her second rotation. Still another child learns first in small-group instruction, but then learns online with a virtual tutor.

This is the Individual Rotation model. Each student has an individualized playlist and does not necessarily rotate to each available station or modality, but all students rotate at a fixed time.

WATCH CLIP 10: The Individual Rotation model at Carpe Diem in Yuma, Arizona, relies on a unique facility and staffing design.

www.wiley.com/go/blended10

Scenario 5

Students in a center take a course online, while an in-person teacher moves around to help them one-on-one or pull them out into small groups when it makes sense to do so.

This is the Flex model. An online course is the backbone of student learning, and students are moving on an individually customized, fluid schedule among learning modalities. The teacher of record is in person.

WATCH CLIP 11: At San Francisco Flex Academy, students learn online and get help on a flexible basis from academic coaches and teachers.

www.wiley.com/go/blended11

Scenario 6

A student takes an AP course online with a virtual teacher for her sixth class of the day at a traditional brick-and-mortar school.

This is the A La Carte model. A student is taking a class entirely online with an online teacher but also learning at a brick-and-mortar school for the rest of the day.

Scenario 7

A student learns online from home three days a week to accommodate her training schedule for ice hockey. The other two days, she learns at a traditional school with her fellow students and teacher.

This is the Enriched Virtual model. The student has required face-to-face learning sessions with her teacher of record but then learns online remotely for the rest of her learning.

WATCH CLIP 12: Henry County Schools in Georgia provide a learning space and face-to-face teachers to enrich students who are taking online courses at Impact Academy.

www.wiley.com/go/blended12

Check for understanding

Which blended model is it?

Here are some opportunities for you to practice identifying which model of blended learning is being used in the different scenarios. The answers and explanations are in the appendix.

1. Aaron Sams uses online learning to teach his students science. Watch this video to see how he does it: www.wiley.com/go/blended8.

   Which model of blended learning is it? ______________________________

   Why?

   ____

   ____

   ____

2. In Spanish class, Zach and Paula spend the first twenty minutes learning about irregular verbs with their whole class. In the next twenty minutes, Zach goes with half the class to the computer lab to practice irregular verbs online; the online program assesses his abilities and sends the results to the teacher. Paula and the other half of the class pair off to practice speaking and listening to irregular verbs. In the final twenty minutes of class, the two groups switch while the teacher uses data from the online program to inform the next day's lesson.

   Which model of blended learning is it? ______________________________

   Why?

   ____

   ____

   ____

3. Destiny has trouble understanding the teacher's lesson on finding the area of a circle. The teacher directs Destiny and a group of students to work on Chromebooks in class, where Destiny solidifies her understanding of a circle's radius through online practice problems. After thirty minutes, another group of students work online while Destiny and her group work with the teacher. After gaining a better foundation of knowledge and with the aid of her teacher, who had gained a sounder understanding of where Destiny's gaps were, Destiny now grasps how to find the area of a circle.

Which model of blended learning is it? ______________________

Why?

____

____

____

4. Naveed has independent work time all Friday morning, during which he chooses how to learn from a variety of online resources that his teachers have compiled about sediment formation. He watches videos and does practice quizzes in class until he feels ready to take an assessment on the topic.

   Which model of blended learning is it? ______________________

   Why?

   ____

   ____

   ____

5. Students work through their online learning playlists during personalized learning time and then complete skills-based projects and collaborative projects facilitated by the teachers in their classes. Watch this video to see how this model looks: www.wiley.com/go/blended17.

   Which model of blended learning is it? ______________________

   Why?

   ____

   ____

   ____

6. Bo's school doesn't offer Chinese, so he takes an online Chinese course in the library with a certified online teacher.

   Which model of blended learning is it? ______________________

   Why?

   ____

   ____

   ____

7. Annie's homeschool co-op meets in person on Mondays and Wednesdays. The other days, the students complete online coursework from home. During the in-person meetings, Annie meets in a small group or individually with the teacher to get help with the online course. She spends the rest of class time either meeting with other students to finish their team project or continuing to work online, depending on her deadlines.

   Which *two* models of blended learning are these? ____________________

   Why?

   ____

   ____

   ____

8. Marco watches his teacher's recorded calculus lecture on his smartphone as homework. The next day at school, his class spends thirty minutes reviewing the online lecture (if necessary) and completing online practice exercises, as well as thirty minutes completing a group project on Riemann sums.

   Which *two* models of blended learning are these? ____________________

   Why?

   ____

   ____

   ____

Apply the learning

Visually represent each blended model

The blended-learning models are classified based on how students move among different learning modalities and on their interaction with their teacher. Drawing—or diagramming—the different models can be a helpful way to deepen your understanding of the models. In the space below, diagram each of the seven different models in whatever way helps you visualize how students experience them. Our diagrams of the models are in Appendix 1.2 in Chapter One of *Blended.*

Apply the learning

When is each model a fit?

Educators often get hung up trying to decide on the "best" model of blended learning. That question is a dead end. A better way to think about it is to consider the types of circumstances that are well suited to a particular model and the types of circumstances in which a model is a bad fit.

Deepen your understanding of the blended-learning models by thinking about that question and filling in the following tables. Try to think of three or four circumstances for each box.

Station Rotation

Imagine a few circumstances in which this model is a good fit	Imagine a few circumstances in which this model is a poor fit
Example: A third-grade teacher has 30 students and wishes she had a way to do small-group instruction.	*Example:* Zack is capable of working twice as fast as the rest of his class in math, but all of the stations in the rotation are for the same math unit.
2.	2.
3.	3.
4.	4.

Lab Rotation

Imagine a few circumstances in which this model is a good fit	Imagine a few circumstances in which this model is a poor fit
1.	1.
2.	2.
3.	3.
4.	4.

Flipped Classroom

Imagine a few circumstances in which this model is a good fit	Imagine a few circumstances in which this model is a poor fit
1.	1.
2.	2.
3.	3.
4.	4.

Individual Rotation

Imagine a few circumstances in which this model is a good fit	Imagine a few circumstances in which this model is a poor fit
1.	1.
2.	2.
3.	3.
4.	4.

Flex

Imagine a few circumstances in which this model is a good fit	Imagine a few circumstances in which this model is a poor fit
1.	1.
2.	2.
3.	3.
4.	4.

A La Carte

Imagine a few circumstances in which this model is a good fit	Imagine a few circumstances in which this model is a poor fit
1.	1.
2.	2.
3.	3.
4.	4.

Enriched Virtual

Imagine a few circumstances in which this model is a good fit	Imagine a few circumstances in which this model is a poor fit
1.	1.
2.	2.
3.	3.
4.	4.

Draft your plan

Plan a two-hour student experience

For each of the models, write out what a two-hour experience might look for a student working in that model. The time does not need to be contiguous or in one setting. To get you started, here's an example:

Example: Station Rotation for grade 3 math

30 minutes—Student learns individually online on ST Math; when she gets stuck, she talks to her friend next to her for help.

30 minutes—Small-group instruction with teacher and fellow students who are working on the same set of math concepts.

30 minutes—Collaborative small-group project in which the student works with physical manipulatives in a group of two others to solve a series of math problems.

30 minutes—The whole class works in small groups of their choice on "math challenges," an activity that stretches the ability of the students in the class to solve fun, real-world problems.

Now it's your turn.

Station Rotation

____

____

____

____

____

____

____

____

Lab Rotation

Flipped Classroom

Individual Rotation

Flex

A La Carte

Enriched Virtual

APPENDIX

Check for understanding: Is it blended?

1. No. Although collaboration tools enable students to work more efficiently together, they don't manage the delivery of content and instruction; the face-to-face teacher does that. The students are still learning the same thing at the same time. They therefore do not have control over the time, place, path, or pace of their learning, so it is not blended learning.
2. No. Although online resources can be valuable additions to the classroom, in this instance the teacher is not using online content to give students individual control over their learning. The students are still learning the same thing at the same time. They therefore do not have control over the time, place, path, or pace of their learning, so it is not blended learning.
3. Yes. Students use the learning resources to control the path of learning; each can master the standards through different means. They also use it to control the pace of learning; when they are ready, they show they have gained mastery through an assessment. This is blended learning.
4. No. Although video games can be effective in engaging students in their learning, in this instance Minecraft is used as a supplemental tool and is not connected to students' other learning experiences, so it is not blended learning.
5. Yes. Students are controlling the pace of their learning online, and the teacher is able to use this data to target instruction, so the online and offline learning experiences are connected. This is blended learning.
6. Yes. Students have control over the over the path and pace of their learning with guidance from a teacher. This is blended learning.

Check for understanding: Which blended model is it?

1. Flipped Classroom. This is the Flipped Classroom model because the student has control over the time and pace of the content delivery. Class time builds off that content.
2. Lab Rotation. This is the Lab Rotation model because the student rotates on a fixed schedule and/or at the teacher's discretion into a computer lab for the online learning component.
3. Station Rotation. This is the Station Rotation model because the student rotates into different stations within the classroom, and all students go to all stations.
4. Flex. This is the Flex model because the student moves on a flexible, fluid, personalized schedule through the learning.
5. Flex. This is the Flex model because the student moves on a flexible, fluid, personalized schedule through the learning.
6. A La Carte. This is the A La Carte model because the student takes a fully online course to accompany a brick-and-mortar experience.
7. Enriched Virtual and Flex. This is in part an Enriched Virtual model because students are required to meet in person with their face-to-face teacher on Mondays and Wednesdays and then are free to complete the rest of the course remote from campus. The in-person class time is a Flex model because the students move on a flexible, fluid schedule based on their needs.
8. Flipped and Station Rotation. This is a Flipped Classroom model because the students control the time and place where they consume the online lecture. During class time, it's a Station Rotation. The students rotate in thirty-minute increments between online learning and project-based learning.

Disruptive Innovation and Blended Learning

Key objectives

- Spot which models of blended learning are hybrid, sustaining innovations of the classroom and which disrupt the classroom
- Explain why this lens matters for a successful implementation

Content summary

Hybrid and disruptive models of blended learning

In Chapter Two of *Blended,* we review how some models of blended learning are sustaining innovations to the traditional classroom; they seek to combine the best of online learning with the best of the traditional classroom to create a *hybrid.*

Other models of blended learning are disruptive relative to the traditional classroom. They do away with the traditional classroom's value propositions and seek to create learning environments unconstrained by its four walls. There is a simple rule of thumb for spotting a disruptive model of blended learning: *if students are learning in a blended setting and you can't figure out where the front of the classroom is, then it's probably a disruptive model.*

The Station Rotation, Lab Rotation, and Flipped Classroom models are important hybrid, sustaining innovations relative to the traditional classroom and are likely to be a mainstay in the American education landscape for years to come. The Individual Rotation, Flex, A La Carte, and Enriched Virtual models are disruptive to the traditional classroom.

Today, the hybrid models of blended learning are the best fit for core academic courses. In contrast, the disruptive models of blended learning are the best fit for areas of *nonconsumption*—where the alternative is no course at all, such as for credit recovery, dropout recovery, unit recovery, or advanced courses that resource-strapped schools in urban and rural environments cannot otherwise offer—or where existing schools are *overserving* learners who are not so complicated to serve well academically, as in many suburban communities in the United States, for example.

Check for understanding

Spotting hybrids and disruptions

How well can you identify whether something is a sustaining hybrid or disruptive? Check your understanding here. The answers are in the appendix for this module.

Circle one:

1. An innovation that uses both the old and new technology is likely a . . .

   Hybrid   Disruption

   Why?

   ____

   ____

2. An innovation that serves nonconsumers is likely a . . .

   Hybrid   Disruption

   Why?

   ____

   ____

3. Students learn in a classroom where a teacher is planning lessons for and lecturing to students every day and also managing students' online learning. This is likely a . . .

   Hybrid   Disruption

   Why?

   ____

   ____

4. Students move on as they master material and can jump between subjects as it makes sense for them. This is likely a . . .

   Hybrid   Disruption

   Why?

   ____

   ____

In the chart here, list each of the following blended-learning models in the most appropriate zone—the Hybrid Zone or the Disruptive Zone—depending on how it is usually implemented:

Station Rotation

Lab Rotation

Flipped Classroom

Individual Rotation

Flex

A La Carte

Enriched Virtual

Hybrid Zone	Disruptive Zone

Content summary

Why disruptive innovation theory matters

Some varieties of blended learning are hybrids of the old and new, and as such they are sustaining innovations. This means that they are poised to build on and offer sustaining enhancements to, but not fundamentally re-architect, the traditional classroom. Schools that are struggling with flat or deteriorating test scores and strained budgets can find relief by harnessing the efficiencies that models such as the Station Rotation, Lab Rotation, and Flipped Classroom bring to the system. Such innovations are critical to advancing learning. Every individual classroom should be seeking to implement sustaining innovations to improve what they currently offer.

Meanwhile, disruptive models of blended learning are on track to replace the traditional system over time at the high school level, and to some extent the middle school level as well. The hybrid models of blended learning will eventually fall by the wayside as the pure disruption becomes good enough over the long term to replace the vestiges of the traditional system.

The pattern of disruptive innovation can take the guesswork out of anticipating the eventual size and scope of the rise of blended learning. It indicates that the future learning environments of high school and middle school, and to some extent elementary school, will be substantially different from the traditional classrooms of today.

School leaders who want to benefit from both sustaining and disruptive innovation should consider a two-part strategy. For the first part, they should implement hybrid models of blended learning to improve their traditional classrooms. For the second part, they should look for opportunities to deploy disruptive models of blended learning to fill gaps in areas of nonconsumption and prepare for the future.

Expand your strategy skills

Imagine that . . .

Practice your strategy skills by imagining yourself in the following circumstances. What should you do? Use your understanding of hybrid and disruptive innovations to arrive at your answer. A discussion of ways to approach these scenarios is in the appendix at the end of this module.

1. Imagine that you are the superintendent of a large urban district in the midwestern United States. You see real possibility in using the Flipped Classroom model to improve your otherwise traditional high school classrooms. But the advice to consider a two-part strategy makes sense. What other initiative could you design to ensure that you are implementing both sustaining and disruptive innovations?

   ____

   ____

   ____

2. Imagine that your community is relatively change resistant. Many of your teachers are concerned about blended learning. What initiative could you design to bring the benefits of a disruptive model of blended learning to an area of nonconsumption, while avoiding raising undue concern among teachers who are serving mainstream students in core classrooms?

   ____

   ____

   ____

3. Imagine that you already have a few disruptive innovations in the works, including a new Enriched Virtual program for students who want the benefits of homeschooling, and a Flex lab for students in the alternative high school. But most of your classrooms are still basically traditional or technology rich, not blended. What would be the easiest way to get started with blended learning in those classrooms, and why?

   ____

   ____

   ____

Draw your conclusions

What are your takeaways?

In the next module, you will assess your interest in and readiness for blended learning. Then, in Part 2 of this workbook, you will dive into designing and planning for your blended-learning implementation. Before you do that, it's wise to step back and cement your thinking about how the vocabulary and theories in Module 1.1 and this module will inform your efforts. Use this space to note any important takeaways that you want to remember as you begin to design and plan.

APPENDIX

Check for understanding: Spotting hybrids and disruptions

1. Hybrid. Hybrid innovations include both the old and new technology, whereas pure disruptions do not offer the old technology in its full form.
2. Disruption. Hybrid innovations target existing customers, whereas disruptions target nonconsumers.
3. Hybrid. Hybrid innovations tend to be more complicated to operate than disruptive innovations and require expertise in both the old and the new.
4. Disruption. Hybrids seek to outperform the existing system according to the old rules of the game, whereas disruptions compete on different terms and offer an alternative set of benefits. Here the disruption is focused on mastery of learning, not seat time.

Hybrid Zone	Disruptive Zone
Station Rotation	Individual Rotation
Lab Rotation	Flex
Flipped Classroom	A La Carte
	Enriched Virtual

Expand your strategy skills: Imagine that . . .

1. The Flipped Classroom is in the Hybrid Zone, so it is a sustaining innovation. You should consider a disruptive innovation to achieve your hope for a two-part strategy. For example, you could pilot a summer school Enriched Virtual math boot camp, introduce a menu of A La Carte online foreign language courses, or open a dropout recovery center that is based on a Flex model.

2. One benefit of starting a disruptive innovation in an area of nonconsumption is that, by starting there, you are unlikely to cause much concern among those in the traditional system. In fact, they might even appear relieved that someone is finally solving the problem! For example, you could develop an A La Carte program for students who are sick or homebound, design a Flex credit recovery program, create a Flex computer coding club for after school, or develop an Individual Rotation model for advanced science courses that the school has never been able to offer before.

3. The easiest way to get started with blended learning in core classrooms that serve mainstream students is through a model in the Hybrid Zone. You could design a pilot to test a Station Rotation, Lab Rotation, or Flipped Classroom experience.

Interest and Readiness Survey

Key objectives

- ○ Survey your team and organization to assess whether your interest and readiness are high enough to begin this work
- ○ Compare your organization to other teams to see whether your interest and readiness levels are on par with teams that went on to develop successful plans
- ○ Take action to improve your readiness

Content summary

Do you have what it takes?

As you dive into blended learning, it helps to know what your own appetite—and the appetite of your team members, organization, or broader community around you—is for innovating. Are you ready for the changes blended learning will bring? What's driving each of you to blend? And how extensive is your vision of change: Are you ready to change one classroom, one school, or an entire network of schools?

These questions are important because teachers and schools juggle countless priorities. It takes deep commitment to put other projects to the side for a time for the sake of transforming classrooms into student-centered environments.

This module offers a survey of questions to help you self-evaluate. In the ideal, you will discuss these questions as a team. Alternatively, have each team member answer independently and then compare the results as a group. The survey is focused on helping you assess a school or system's readiness for and interest in innovating. If you are working alone to blend a single classroom, then you already know your own level of interest, and the questions are less applicable; nonetheless, you may find that they help you reflect on the effort that will be required. If you are contemplating school- or system-wide change, then the questions will help you understand whether you're ready to dive into the rest of the workbook or whether you need to spend more time educating your colleagues, building capacity, or communicating a rich vision that brings on board the stakeholders needed to support a wider initiative.

We thank the Highlander Institute, whose interview questions to select schools for the FUSE Rhode Island blended-learning project contributed to this survey.[1]

Expand your strategy skills

Begin the survey

For questions 1–13, enter a numeric score according to the scale provided in the second column. Questions 14–20 are open-ended questions. Write your responses and then use the rubric that follows the survey to score your responses. At the end, total all the numbers in the second column to arrive at a composite score.

Interest and Readiness Survey	Score
Planning questions **1 = Not a priority** **2 = Somewhat interested** **3 = Current area of discussion or implementation** **4 = Top priority** **5 = Area of strength**	
1. Where does blended learning fit within your current school- or system-level strategic plan?	
2. What is your interest in providing all students with a learning environment that is fully personalized to their needs and abilities?	
3. What is your interest in running individual classroom pilots to demonstrate blended learning?	
4. What is your interest in running school-wide and/or system-wide pilots to demonstrate blended learning?	
5. What is your school's—or school system's—willingness to develop new policies and administrative competencies to facilitate blended learning?	
6. How interested is your school or school system in reworking daily schedules and operations to design a more effective student experience?	
7. How interested is your school or school system in adjusting teachers' professional development plans to support them in the process of blended-learning implementation?	
8. Where does data collection and analysis fall among your current priorities?	
9. How ready are key stakeholders—such as school board members, the superintendent, the district leadership team, principals, teachers, the teacher's union, and parents—to support a blended-learning demonstration initiative at your school(s)?	

Interest and Readiness Survey	Score
10. How ready are you to provide Wi-Fi, bandwidth, and tech support to ensure that a strong infrastructure is in place, either because of existing resources or willingness and ability to redirect resources?	
11. What is your personal willingness to carve out significant time over the next six months to develop a blended-learning plan, ideally with a team?	
12. What is your overall interest in being a model for others to demonstrate the benefits of well-designed blended learning within three years?	
Autonomy question **1 = Strongly disagree** **2 = Somewhat disagree** **3 = Unsure** **4 = Somewhat agree** **5 = Strongly agree**	
13. On a 1–5 scale, do you agree that you and/or your team has enough **autonomy** to change the fundamental design of your classroom(s) over the next three to five years? Autonomy can include the power to adjust the bell schedules, reallocate a portion of the budget, modify the deployment of teachers and change their professional development plans, and design a different approach to curriculum. Note that this question is about autonomy and power, not about time and money!	
Open-ended questions **Score these on a 1–5 scale, according to the Open-Ended Questions Rubric in the following worksheet.**	
14. **Goals.** Why are you interested in blended learning? What are you hoping to achieve for students?	

Interest and Readiness Survey	Score
15. **Team.** For questions 15–19, each team member should state why he or she is committed to participating in this initiative. (If you are completing this survey alone or with fewer than five team members, skip questions as necessary.) Team member 1 response:	
16. Team member 2 response:	
17. Team member 3 response:	
18. Team member 4 response:	
19. Team member 5 response:	
20. **Project manager.** Do you already have a project manager to lead this work? If so, describe at least one time when the project manager worked entrepreneurially to overcome obstacles and launch a new project or initiative. If not, do you have the resources to hire a project manager or to be the project manager yourself?	
Total Score (Add up all your points)	
Total Points Possible	**100**

Finished!

Analyze your work

Self-assess your responses to the open-ended questions

The following is a rubric to help you score your responses to the open-ended questions in the survey. It distinguishes an answer that evidences little interest in and readiness for implementing blended learning (1 point) from one that evidences advanced interest and readiness (5 points). Use this rubric to assign scores to Questions 14–20 in the survey.

Open-Ended Questions Rubric

Question	Advanced interest and readiness 5	Strong interest and readiness 4	Moderate interest and readiness 3	Basic interest and readiness 2	Little interest and readiness 1
14: Goals	Shows **exceptional** understanding of what blended learning is and an **expansive, but fully realistic,** vision for what it can achieve	Shows **familiarity** with blended learning and an **emerging, mostly realistic** vision for what it can achieve	Shows **adequate** understanding of what blended learning is and **some ideas** for what it might achieve	Shows **beginning** understanding of what blended learning is and **an unclear/ mostly unrealistic** vision for what it can achieve	Shows **little** understanding of what blended learning is, and the vision for what it can achieve is **absent or unrealistic**
15–19: Team	Evidences **passion** and **full commitment**	Evidences **strong interest** and **some commitment**	Evidences **moderate interest** and **some commitment**, along with other priorities	Evidences **some interest,** second to other priorities	Evidences **reluctance**

Question	Advanced interest and readiness 5	Strong interest and readiness 4	Moderate interest and readiness 3	Basic interest and readiness 2	Little interest and readiness 1
20: Project manager	Shows that a **deeply** experienced, entrepreneurial project manager has been hired or will be hired soon	Shows that a **somewhat** experienced, entrepreneurial project manager has been hired or will be hired soon	Likelihood of having an experienced, entrepreneurial project manager is **probable, but not definite**	Likelihood of having an experienced, entrepreneurial project manager is **possible, but uncertain**	**Does not show potential** for having an experienced, entrepreneurial project manager

View benchmarks

Sample answers to open-ended questions

The examples here are actual responses from administrators and teachers who completed this survey and went on to successfully implement full blended-learning programs. Although there are no single right answers, these examples may be helpful to you as you calibrate your own position.

1. Goals: Why are you interested in blended learning? What are you hoping to achieve for students?

   Sample 1: In our location as a small, rural district, we see around us daily the evidence of the importance of readying our students for a dynamic world, driven by science, technology, and mathematics. Standardized assessments are not enough; instead, we must effectively integrate cutting-edge tools and student independence with competency-based learning. We envision a flexible learning environment where students' needs are met based upon the individual and which is undergirded by a well-trained, passionate faculty. We want evidence of improvement in score results as well as true student understanding, motivation, and preparation for the future.

   Sample 2: At our district, with a student population of 62,373 high-need students in grades PK–12, in which 79 percent are Hispanic, 81 percent qualify for the free and reduced lunch program, and 51 percent are considered at-risk of dropping out of school or academic failure, we have difficulty overcoming academic challenges using traditional instructional methods. Thus, our district is approaching these challenges with a blended-learning model that will lead to student success by providing teachers answers to four critical questions in order to individualize instruction: (1) What do we expect our students to learn? (2) How will we know when they have learned it? (3) How will we respond when some students do not learn? (4) How will we respond when some students already know it?

Sample 3: The tremendous diversity of our population in terms of culture, economic status, level of education, and educational goals demands that we differentiate learning much more than we are currently able to. We need to leverage the efficiency that technology brings to ensure all students maximize learning in a way that is meaningful to them. We are convinced that the blended-learning model is the only model that meets the students where they are and creates a partnership with the student, parent, and teacher that distributes learning that is personalized and effective.

2. Team: Why is each of your team members committed to participating in this initiative?

   Sample 1: Competency-based projects are common at the college level, where I have worked extensively, and are effective for helping students and teachers to feel empowered and successful. This feeling of success based on mastery empowers students of all ages. Finding effective integration methods for technology excites me!

   Sample 2: My job is to make certain our district makes the most effective use of funds for the betterment of our students. We must be good stewards of resources. Being part of this team to consider new instruction methods allows me to plan and ensure the sustainability of programs.

   Sample 3: I began researching blended learning about a year ago. The more I explored, the more I knew it had the potential to impact students in ways we'd never seen in our classrooms. Implementing blended learning in our district is the next logical step in fostering student success.

   Sample 4: Blending learning extends learning to anyone, anywhere, anytime. Confining learning to a classroom with the perceived expert disseminating information is no longer a viable instructional model. Students today crave being in control of their learning. Blended learning provides opportunities for individualized, self-paced, on-the-go learning. As Superintendent, it is my goal to lead the blended-learning initiative in our district, region, and state.

3. Project manager: Describe at least one time when the project manager worked entrepreneurially to overcome obstacles and launch a new project or initiative.

   Sample 1: I have served on numerous grant and academic change teams as a director, with plans ranging from restructuring entire academic programs to creating scalable programs for other programs. The projects were massive, involving so many people that at times they seemed impossible. Resistance to change was a major factor, but I found that educating the stakeholders was the key to their buy-in and our ultimate success. Communicate with and educate the people involved—give them a voice for concerns and for ideas. It was fulfilling to see that our efforts led to better educational approaches for students and to the receiving of vital funding for key projects.

   Sample 2: In my role as a principal tasked with opening a new elementary school in my district, my primary goals were to open the school on time, demonstrate student achievement through successful student assessment scores, and to serve as a model for future elementary schools. During this process, I faced considerable challenges such as overseeing construction and selecting and purchasing all furniture, technology, and curriculum. One of the largest challenges I faced was recruiting and hiring staff, along with designing the curriculum and staff development for the first year. My work managing the opening of this school resulted in the establishment of an academically successful elementary school model used district-wide.

Sample 3: Collaborating with our city's respective government entities to extend the reach of our city's free broadband into all our district's poorest neighborhoods and the students who live there has been a challenge. Highlighting the advantages of a seamless mesh of Wi-Fi with benefits for city and community entities while navigating the potential political landmines was fraught with setbacks. Taking the lead for this initiative, I have worked with the various groups to agree to the benefits and continue to work on the logistics of who owns and maintains the system, etc. The momentum has resulted in a pilot project that was installed this spring and full launch is planned for the fall.

Draw your conclusions

How can you prepare?

Review your points and responses on your survey and answer these reflection questions.

1. What are your organization's three to five areas of strength with regard to its collective interest in and readiness for implementing blended learning?

2. What are your organization's three to five area of weakness or liabilities with regard to its collective interest in and readiness for implementing blended learning?

3. What action steps should a coalition of willing members of your organization take to improve the collective interest and readiness?

4. Based on the time required to complete the action steps you listed in Question 3, what is the best time frame for your team to begin to design and then to implement your blended-learning plan?

____

____

____

____

____

____

Note

1. Highlander Institute's FUSE Rhode Island interview questions are available here: bit.ly/BlendedInterviewQues. Used with permission of Highlander Institute under the terms of its Creative Commons License.

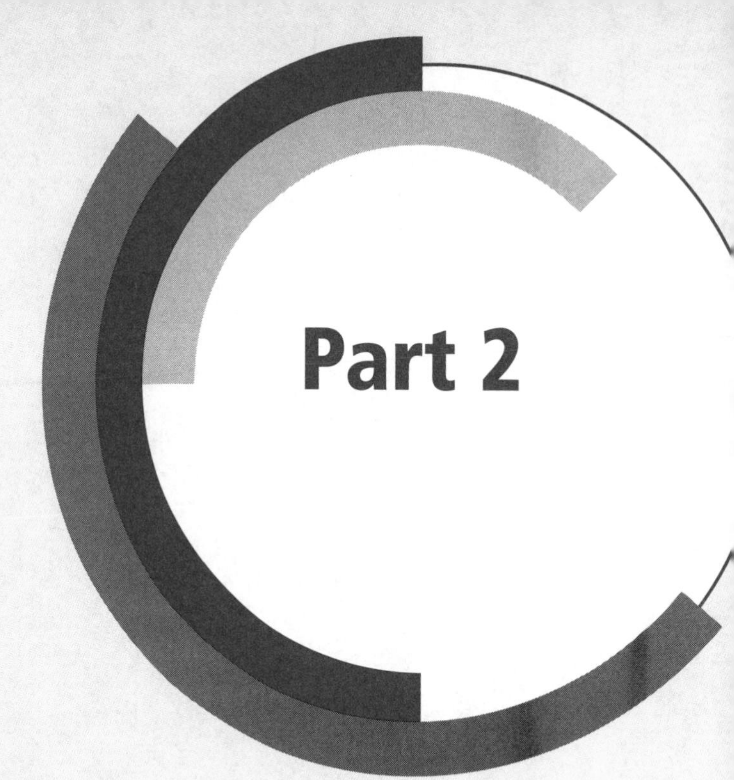

Developing Your Plan

Rallying Cry

Key objectives

- ○ Begin building your blended-learning plan
- ○ Identify and articulate the school's most important problems that blended learning can help solve
- ○ Develop goals that make technology subordinate to a higher goal and that are specific, measurable, assignable, realistic, and time-related (SMART)

Content summary

Begin with a plan

Schools feel pressure to invest in technology. Students carry devices in their pockets and use them whenever and wherever they can. Teachers hear about new products and wonder if anything might help a struggling or disengaged child in their class. Administrators, who feel pressure to produce blue-ribbon results on a shoestring budget, wonder if technology could give them a boost.

Coordinating technology investments across these stakeholders is difficult. The various users want different things. At the teacher level, student and teacher needs vary from classroom to classroom. At the administrative level, technology specialists, curriculum specialists, and the finance team see the world differently. Furthermore, products are frequently updated; refreshing them in a unified cadence can be complicated. In short, the job of managing software, systems, and devices in schools is troublesome. Over time, many districts find themselves in a big tech mess.

When it comes to technology, schools need a blended-learning plan. A blended-learning plan is a written document that describes how an organization is going to achieve its goals as it invests in technology. It provides the road map for how the parts of the operation—from the facilities and faculty to the culture and budgets—will work together toward a unified objective.

Part 2 of this workbook walks you through the steps for writing a complete blended-learning plan to design and implement blended learning. You can draft each section of your plan here in the workbook—or we've also provided a way for you to work on a digital copy of the blended-learning plan template using Google Docs.

To work on your plan as a Google Doc, go to bit.ly/BlendedPlanTemplate and click on the "Make a copy" icon. A new page will open with your own copy of the blended-learning plan template that we use in this workbook.

Part 3 of this workbook includes the complete blended-learning plan template to provide you with an offline copy of the planning document in one place.

Identify problems

The most successful blended-learning programs begin by identifying the problem to solve. This starting point might at first seem obvious, but a glance at major education purchases in recent years shows that the temptation to lead with the technology is pervasive. Too many schools invest big dollars in one-to-one programs without a clear statement of intent about what all that computing power will accomplish. They invest in "technology for technology's sake," rather than in technology for the sake of achieving an important set of student or school outcomes.

One consideration when identifying the problem to solve is whether blended learning is the right tool. Don't choose problems for which blended learning has no answer. For example, blended learning has not proven effective in ensuring that students have safe transportation to school or improving the school lunch menu. Blended learning is a better fit for problems related to (1) boosting student achievement and quality of life through personalizing learning, (2) providing students more ownership over their work to bolster motivation and develop student agency, (3) freeing up teachers' time to serve as individual coaches, (4) providing access to out-of-reach courses and opportunities, (5) improving a school system's financial health, or (6) various combinations of these goals.

When brainstorming problem statements, be sure to explore two aspects of your operations. First, consider problems that affect your **mainstream students and teachers in core subjects.** It's likely that you already have a full program in place for these classrooms, but the classrooms could benefit from innovations that help them serve students better. Such circumstances present fertile opportunities for educators to implement sustaining innovations using blended learning.

Second, discuss problems related to **areas of nonconsumption**. Nonconsumption exists any time that schools cannot provide a learning experience; they have no easy option other than to do without it. Schools often discover that blended learning allows them to offer new services that before were out of reach.

Look for opportunities to improve your schools by solving problems in both categories: core problems that affect mainstream students in core subjects, and nonconsumption problems that affect those who find themselves left out of learning opportunities altogether. As you articulate these problems, be sure to provide baseline data to quantify their size before the new changes take place. Baseline data helps you measure the magnitude of your improvement.

Prioritize problems

Some schools find that their list of problems is long. For the purpose of writing a blended-learning plan, how should schools home in on the top priorities? Different people, organizations, and schools will come up with different ways to decide where to start. Legend has it that President Eisenhower sorted his workload and priorities by ranking them according to their urgency and importance. The so-called Eisenhower Principle states that leaders should tackle problems in this order:

1. Important and urgent
2. Important but not urgent
3. Not important but urgent
4. Not important and not urgent

Consider ranking problems according to their importance and urgency as you select the one or two that are the most worthy of your effort with blended learning. But one note: be sure to rank your core and nonconsumption problems separately, or else the opportunity to innovate in areas of nonconsumption will almost always fall by the wayside as the problems there often feel, at most, important but not necessarily urgent.

Student-centered innovators who begin by articulating a clear, high-priority set of core and nonconsumption problems to tackle have an advantage over technology purchasers who begin with a hardware and software wish list. The student-centered innovators have a vision for what they want to improve in their students' lives, and that aspiration anchors their decisions going forward.

Check for understanding

Avoid the technology trap

Review the list of problem statements below. **Circle** the one that focuses the most on student or school outcomes instead of on a lack of technology. Then answer the reflection question. Our answer is in the appendix at the end of this module.

School's problem statements

1. Most students who are part of the free and reduced-price lunch program do not have their own devices.
2. Fifty-three percent of classrooms are still using paper textbooks instead of interactive digital textbooks.
3. Administrators rely on an outdated student information system.
4. Upper elementary school teachers do not have electronic whiteboards.
5. Four classrooms must share a single laptop cart.
6. Professional development is being delivered using 20th-century tools.
7. English language learners enter ninth grade two grade levels behind in math.
8. Students do not have equal access to Wi-Fi at home.
9. Teachers must supply their own phones and devices.
10. The district does not have a unified learning management system.

Reflection question

How does focusing on student or school outcomes instead of on access to technology help schools develop a better strategy for purchasing technology?

____

____

____

____

Brainstorm the options

Identify core and nonconsumption problems

Most schools already have comprehensive programs in place for basic reading, math, and science education, but the classrooms could benefit from innovations that help them serve students better. Use the space below to list core problems that hold back your students. Resist identifying low test scores as the problem. Instead, think about instructional gaps, environmental barriers, and other root problems that prevent achievement. Test scores can indicate that there is a problem or that the problem is resolved, but they are not the problem itself. They are a symptom. The following are examples of core problems:

- Kindergarteners and transfer students enter the district with wide disparities in reading skills.
- High school teachers do not have time to give individual feedback on writing assignments.
- Observational data and student surveys show that many high school students are bored in class.
- Middle school students lack the family support to complete take-home projects.

Your core problems:

1. ______________________________
2. ______________________________
3. ______________________________
4. ______________________________
5. ______________________________
6. ______________________________
7. ______________________________
8. ______________________________
9. ______________________________
10. ______________________________

Nonconsumption arises any time schools cannot provide a learning experience; they have no easy option other than to do without it. Brainstorm the most significant nonconsumption problems within your school. The following are examples of nonconsumption problems:

- A number of students have dropped out of school.
- Students do not have a realistic way to recover units and credits to stay on track for graduation.
- Students do not have access to the electives they want or need.
- The school does not offer speech or behavioral therapy.
- Students do not have access to SAT/ACT test preparation.
- Students develop learning gaps because they miss school for extracurricular activities.

Your nonconsumption problems:

1. ______________________________
2. ______________________________
3. ______________________________
4. ______________________________
5. ______________________________
6. ______________________________
7. ______________________________
8. ______________________________
9. ______________________________
10. ______________________________

Expand your strategy skills

Urgent/Important Matrix

The Eisenhower Principle can help you prioritize your list of problems by sorting them according to how important and urgent they are. The Urgent/Important Matrix assists with this sorting task. It contains four quadrants.

Quadrant 1: Important and urgent

Quadrant 2: Important but *not* urgent

Quadrant 3: Not important but urgent

Quadrant 4: Not important and not urgent

Solve the problems in Quadrant 1 first. They are critical to your success and must get done right away. Next, get Quadrant 3 problems out of the way, as they are urgent. Then tackle Quadrant 2 problems, given that they are important and deserve attention. Finally, work on Quadrant 4 problems if time allows.

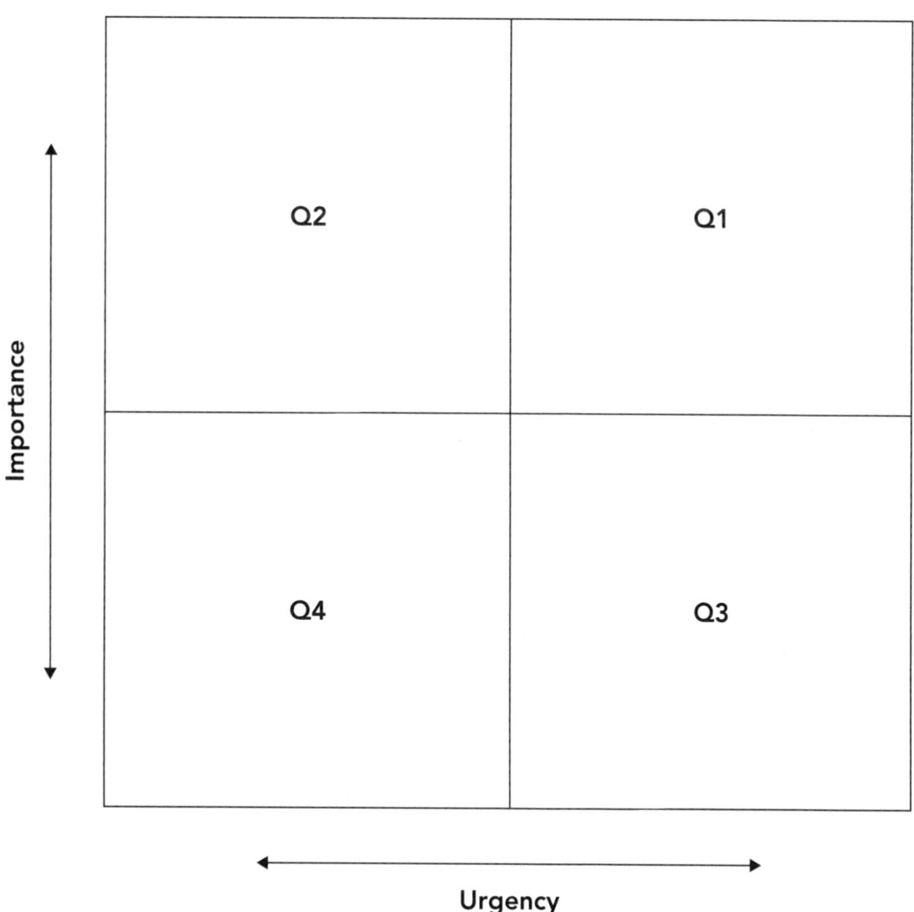

Evaluate the lists of core and nonconsumption problems you brainstormed in the previous step. Within those two categories, write each problem in the appropriate quadrant of the Urgent/Important Matrix by considering these questions:

1. How important is the problem? If it is critical to your organization's goals and values, then it will appear in Q1 or Q2.
2. How urgent is the problem? If it demands immediate attention, then it will appear in Q3 or Q4.

Urgent/Important Matrix

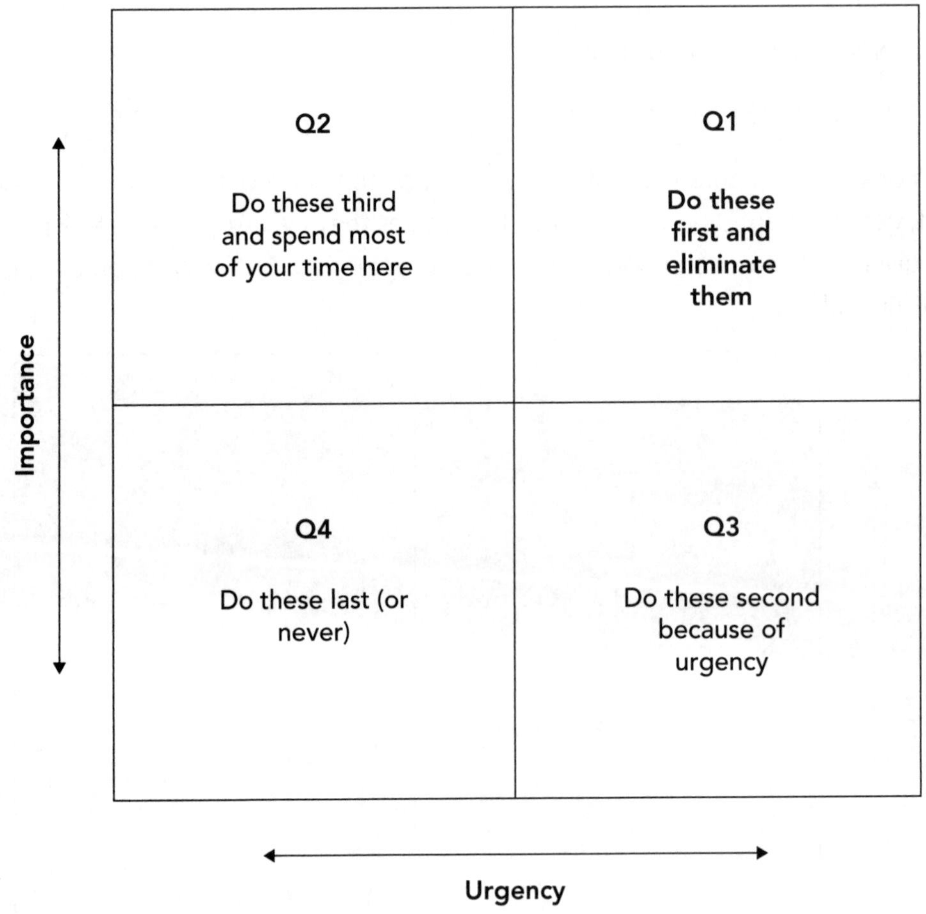

View rubric and benchmarks

Sample problem statements

In the previous exercises, you brainstormed and prioritized problems to solve with blended learning. Before crafting these into complete problem statements, let's view a rubric that points out the differences between an inadequate and an exceptional problem statement. Rubrics assist in the process of developing a strong blended-learning plan—or any other written document, for that matter—because they help the writer gain perspective about what a successful final product looks like. Throughout this workbook, we provide rubrics to help you evaluate your progress.

The rubric here will help you develop and evaluate your problem statement. It distinguishes an inadequate problem statement (0) from one that is basic (1), advanced (2), or exceptional (3). Exceptional plans focus on a top-priority core problem and/or nonconsumption problem. They provide baseline data to quantify the size of the problem. They do not lead with the need for technology for technology's sake. Instead, they identify a student-centered problem that technology may be able to help fix. The technology is subordinate to a more important mission.

Read through the two examples of core problem statements we include here, which are based on statements that real teachers or teams developed. After each statement, we provide our evaluation according to the rubric.

Problem Statement Rubric

Exceptional 3	Advanced 2	Basic 1	Inadequate 0
Identifies at least one core problem and/or one nonconsumption problem. *Requirements:* • Either goes deep by solving one root problem or goes wide by undertaking more than one project to address instructional gaps and/or environmental barriers. • Problem is based on barriers to achievement • Uses quantitative data to show that the problem is significant. • Problem does not focus on "technology for technology's sake"; rather, technology is subordinate to a student-centered mission.	Identifies at least one problem, but is **less than convincing** with one or more of the requirements (e.g., includes quantitative data, but data is not used to illustrate the significance of the problem).	Identifies at least one problem, but **clearly fails to satisfy one to two of the requirements** (e.g., does not include quantitative data).	The answer **does not identify a clear academic problem,** or the statement does not meet **any** of the requirements.

Sample problem statement 1

I have been teaching 10th-grade Chemistry for eight years. I've worked hard to develop engaging lesson plans and informative presentations to teach the standards. On average, only 8 percent of students fail the class each year, which is pretty good for our school. But student engagement is not as high as I would like. Only 55 percent of students agree with the statement: "My chemistry class makes me interested in continuing to study science." I think the problem is that we do not have enough time for wet labs during class. We only have time to do three per semester because of the time that it takes for me to teach the basic content; but I believe students would be more engaged and discover a love of science if they were to do hands-on experiments and active learning *every day.* Furthermore, I do not have time to coach each student to success. Only 29 percent agree with the statement: "My teacher cares about my individual success and gives me the feedback I need to improve my performance." I think the problem is that I do not have time to give them much individual feedback. I seldom (roughly once per semester for 10 percent of the students) meet with my students one-on-one, and I never give much meaningful written feedback. Ultimately, even though the failure rate of 8 percent of my class is low, I would like for it to get to zero.

Scoring explanation

We give this statement 3 points according to the rubric. The teacher has two hypotheses about why engagement is low: not enough time for hands-on labs, and students aren't getting much personal feedback or mentoring from him. He uses baseline data from student surveys and his own record keeping to take the temperature of his classroom prior to making any changes. That will allow him to measure improvement. He says nothing about technology; this problem statement focuses solely on students and their learning needs. His statement shows that he has thought deeply about the gaps and missed opportunities that he suspects are holding back students from greater science achievement.

Sample problem statement 2

Historically, our district has had strong academic performance. As our student population has become more diverse, however, the performance gap is widening, particularly in middle school math. We are struggling to serve our middle school students with disabilities and our English Language Learners (ELL)—and these populations are growing. We believe the root problem for our middle school students with disabilities is that they do not have multiple pathways for mastering the math standards;

observational data shows that 92 percent of the time, all of the students in each middle school math classroom are engaged in the same activities and assignments as the others in their classroom. There is little variation based on ability and needs. We believe the root problem for our middle school students who are ELL is that most of their math instruction is available only in English and is verbally oriented. One hundred percent of math instruction is available in English only and uses challenging English vocabulary, and 82 percent of the lesson plans ask for verbal responses, instead of nonverbal interactions. As a result of both of these problems, we have double-digit achievement gaps within these two groups. Our most recent state test results show that 89 percent of all students met performance standards; however, only 60 percent of our middle school students receiving special education services and 58 percent of our middle school ELL population met performance standards in math.

Scoring explanation

This district's plan goes deep in identifying its core problems related to teaching math to its middle school students with disabilities and its ELL population. It uses quantitative data to show how big the instructional problems are. It does not say that test scores are the problem; instead, it puts the blame on instructional barriers that are preventing students from achieving on state tests. The district focuses on the students and their needs, rather than on technology gaps. We give this statement 3 points according to the rubric.

Practice evaluating

Score these problem statements

Now it's your turn. Rate the following problem statements on a 0–3 scale (0 = inadequate, 1 = basic, 2 = advanced, 3 = exceptional) using the Problem Statement Rubric. Explain your reasons why. Our answers are in the appendix at the end of this module.

Problem statement 1

Whereas 82 percent of high-income students complete college, only 8 percent of low-income students graduate. In today's competitive global economy, a college degree is the key to a life of choice and a chance to improve economic success. At our district, although 89 percent of students matriculate into college, only 54 percent graduate. Studies show if a student takes an advanced placement (AP) course, she is more likely to graduate from college within four years. A university study of students from low-income backgrounds who enrolled in College Algebra found that nearly one-fifth of students withdrew from or failed the class. Those students had low attendance, did not retake quizzes or use the free tutoring service, and failed to complete extra credit or homework. We understand that we must build student agency and resourcefulness intentionally so that all our students are prepared for self-directed learning in college and beyond; this is an opportunity for us as a district to reflect and grow.

We see an opportunity to change our students' college graduation and life success outcomes by focusing on the math pathway, as it has a clearly delineated progression of skills, is the foundation for all STEM disciplines, and is a challenge area for our students enrolled in college. Currently, only 28 percent of our district's high school students enroll in AP Calculus or Statistics. To reach AP math without taking double math or skipping courses, students must complete Algebra I in eighth grade. Currently, only 60 percent of our district's eighth graders do, mainly because they are not academically prepared. Their learning gaps coming into middle school are too disparate for the teacher to remediate in a whole-group setting. Furthermore, a survey from 2016 showed that only 22 percent of students in 12th grade say that their school teaches them agency by letting them drive their own learning. We see an opportunity in blended learning to help students develop the academic skills and agency to succeed on the path to and through college.

Your score: ______________________

Why?

____

____

Problem statement 2

The desire to bring personalization to all students in our district is driven by data made available from the state accountability system and the National Student Clearinghouse annual report. Although 87 percent of our students are graduating from high school, the majority are not graduating from high school ready for postsecondary education. Only 57 percent of our graduating seniors are entering college in the fall immediately after high school, and a mere 24 percent of the students are completing a degree from a postsecondary institution within six years. This data reveals that our students have the academic skills necessary to graduate from high school but may not have some of the personal skills necessary, such as perseverance, self-management, and decision-making skills. In addition, state and district-level data indicates that 4th-grade students are achieving writing success on the state assessment; however, there is a significant decline in their results by 7th grade. Our students need to be empowered to maintain and even increase all the way through to high school graduation (and beyond) the momentum they established in their earliest years of learning at school in our district.

Your score: ______________________

Why?

Problem statement 3

Our district is based in a rural area without consistent access to Wi-Fi and technology. Most of our students do not have devices at home, and our district of 200 students provides only one device for every 4 students, on average. Our teachers have not had very much professional development in how to use devices successfully in their classrooms. Sometimes they resort to scanning their lesson plans into PDFs and posting them online because they do not know where to find engaging content or how to personalize to each student. A recent survey of our teachers showed that only 45 percent of them feel comfortable doing blended learning in their classrooms, and 25 percent of them said that they need more training to be able to troubleshoot when they have technology problems. We seek as a district to empower more of our students by providing them with access to blended learning.

Your score: ______________________________

Why?

____

____

____

____

____

____

Draft your plan

Articulate your problem statement

Now it's your turn. The Rallying Cry section is the first major content section for your blended-learning plan. The purpose of the section is to introduce your plan with a clear problem statement that your school community can rally around with conviction and dedication. Kick off the Rallying Cry section with a brief paragraph of context about your organization, in case you ask readers outside of your organization to critique your plan. Then articulate the problem(s) that your blended-learning program will address.

Specifically, these are the two sets of questions for you to answer:

1. **Context.** Provide a few sentences of context about your district, charter management organization, or school [collectively referred to as "site"]. This may include basic information like the site's location, size, and number of schools, as well as baseline data around academic, athletic, or other extracurricular successes and continued struggles. The idea is to provide enough context such that your problem statement will be rooted within your context, so that you can design a plan appropriate for your circumstances.

   ____

   ____

   ____

   ____

   ____

   ____

   ____

   ____

   ____

   ____

2. **Problem(s).** State the top problem related to student achievement that you intend for student-centered learning to solve. Use baseline data to quantify the problem. You may include more than one problem. You may include both a core and a nonconsumption problem.

   Note: If you are choosing more than one problem to focus on, such as one core problem and one nonconsumption problem, name each initiative as Project 1, Project 2, and so forth for easy reference throughout the rest of your plan. **Important: as we move**

forward in the book, every time we work through an exercise, you should do it for each of the projects you are tackling so that you create a comprehensive plan for each one. Going forward, we won't explicitly reference this for the most part, but will assume that you will tackle each project in each planning exercise.

Project 1

Project 2 (if applicable)

If you plan to address more than two problems, use the blank sheets at the end of the workbook to compose a problem statement for each project.

Before moving on, remember to self-assess your work. Look at the Problem Statement Rubric and see how you'd score yourself. Make any adjustments as necessary.

Content summary

Developing SMART goals

Your problem statement articulates where you are today. Now consider this: Where do you want to be in five years as a result of your blended-learning effort? Let's tackle that question next.

The SMART goal framework is a helpful way to think about goal setting. According to George T. Duran, one of the first to write about SMART goals, organizations should consider the following criteria when designing objectives:

Specific—Does it target a specific area for improvement?

Measurable—Does it quantify or at least suggest an indicator of progress?

Assignable—Who will be responsible?

Realistic—Can results be achieved realistically, given available resources?

Time-related—When can the results be achieved?

Although the task of assigning the project to the right leader may need to wait until the next step of organizing the team (which we discuss in Module 2.3), the practice of setting a SMART rallying cry up front helps schools bring their blended-learning aspirations into sharper resolution.

View rubric and benchmarks

Sizing up SMART goals

To craft a strong statement of what success in solving the problem would look like, state your SMART goal for each problem. Be sure to provide metrics that show where you are now and where you are aiming to be each year. Your SMART goal doesn't have to project out five years, but it often helps to look at least a couple years out into the future and establish some interim goals as well.

The SMART Goals Rubric distinguishes an inadequate SMART goal (0) from a basic SMART goal (1), advanced SMART goal (2), and an exceptional SMART goal (3).

SMART Goals Rubric

Exceptional 3	Advanced 2	Basic 1	Inadequate 0
States a goal that is specific, measurable, assignable, realistic, and time-related (SMART). *Requirements:* • Uses numbers to quantify the improvement that the team plans to achieve. • Identifies specific metrics for Year 1, Year 2, and Year 3, with more narrow, formative, groundwork-laying metrics in the early years and broader, longer-lead-time metrics in the later years. • Sequences these targets in a realistic way, so as not to assume that broad gains in student achievement will happen in Year 1. • Can be assigned to the right leader when the time comes.	States a SMART goal, but **does not meet one requirement.**	States a SMART goal, but **does not meet two to three requirements**.	Does not state a goal **OR** states a goal that does not meet the requirements.

Read through the following example of a real SMART goal that a school team developed in response to one of its problem statements, followed by our evaluation of the goal statement according to the rubric.

Sample SMART goal

Our goal is to meet the needs and aspirations of each learner through an array of personalized-learning opportunities to empower them to set, track, and achieve their goals.

- Year 1: One hundred percent of students, teachers, and staff at all four pilot schools in our district will articulate their personal goals for the week and review their progress each week toward achievement of their goals. Currently, roughly 20 percent of students and teachers at these sites do this. Fifty percent of learners will receive a "3" or better on one or more performance tasks, up from 40 percent.
- Year 2: The goal-setting culture of Year 1 will continue at 100 percent levels. Also, observational data will show that teachers have improved by 30 percentage points in their average scores related to their ability to provide personalized-learning structures that allow students to set, track, and achieve their goals independently, without teachers micromanaging them. The average baseline score now is 32/100, and we want that to grow to 62/100. Seventy percent of learners will receive a "3" or better on one or more performance tasks.
- Year 3: The new processes from Year 1 and Year 2 will extend to all schools in the district, and baseline scores on average will grow to 82/100. Ninety percent of learners will receive a "3" or better on one or more performance tasks. Students in grades 3, 7, and 11 will show 20 percent growth toward proficiency on state exams compared to Year 1.

The associate superintendent for curriculum and instruction will lead this project.

Scoring explanation

This district does a great job of thinking about a mix of metrics that it can use to track whether it is getting closer to its ultimate goal of cultivating self-directed learners who meet their individual goals. It has broken its quantifiable SMART goals into annual targets that show how its progress becomes wider and bigger over time; it also provides baseline data to show where it is now. The targets are sequenced in a realistic way, not assuming broad gains in the first year of implementation, but also planning for significant gains over the three years. We give this statement 3 points.

Practice evaluating

Score these SMART goals

Rate the following SMART goals on a 0–3 scale (0 = inadequate, 1 = basic, 2 = advanced, 3 = exceptional) using the SMART Goals Rubric. Explain your reasons why. Our answers are in the appendix at the end of this module.

Statement 1

Academic Goals: By the end of Year 3 of the pilot program, 85 percent or more of our students will successfully complete Algebra I in 8th grade and, each year, 90 percent of that cohort will successfully complete the next course in the advanced math sequence. This will allow them to be academically prepared for college-level rigor. (Current statistics: 60 percent of our students complete Algebra I in 8th grade; 76 percent of that cohort successfully complete the next course. Although we have evidence from our one-year trial program for dramatic improvement in Year 1, we plan for incremental completion and mastery rates over the three years of the blended-learning initiative.)

Student Agency: Each year of the math pathway, students will show at least a 25 percent increase in indicators of student agency as identified on our age-specific rubric. The college-readiness behaviors they develop in an in-class Flipped Classroom model (i.e., time management, academic self-awareness, seeking and receiving targeted help, etc.) will set them up for success in college.

Implementation: Within three years, the Project Manager and Blended Learning Coach will create a commonly owned plan for success in implementing an in-class Flipped Classroom that can be adapted by other schools in our district and other interested parties for their schools as a framework for innovation.

*Note on measures of success: While the above goals can be tracked within our district during the project, the first cohort's college graduation data will be available, at earliest, in 2024. Our district has identified research-based proxy variables during the three-year implementation period by which we will measure projected college completion: (1) By 10th grade, each student will be on track to graduate from high school in four years with no credit recovery, and (2) By 11th grade, students will score 19 or higher on the ACT.

Your score: ______________________

Why?

___

___

Statement 2

Our district will increase reading scores and postsecondary readiness indicators in all pilot level grades with the objective of increasing the six-year graduation rate across our district. A variety of postsecondary readiness measures, including a self-awareness survey, P-SAT scores, and postsecondary readiness index scores, will be used to indicate growth toward postsecondary readiness. Specific SMART goals are:

- By the end of two years of the initiative, P-SAT scores for participating ninth-grade students will increase by an average of 10 percent.
- In Year 3 and Year 4 of the initiative, P-SAT scores will increase by an average of 5 percent per year.
- Annually, the postsecondary readiness student achievement index score in two or more subjects will increase by 2 percentage points for participating students.
- To raise student postsecondary self-awareness, a survey of cognitive skills and habits of success will be administered to participating students. Postsecondary coaching will take place throughout the year, and we anticipate a gain of +1 on the postsecondary self-awareness survey. An example: students rating themselves as 1 in the cognitive skill of inquiry in the first fall of the initiative would rate themselves as a 2 at the end of spring of the first year.
- Annually, summative reading scores will increase by 3 percent each year.

Your score: ______________________

Why?

Statement 3

Our district will implement a 1:1 initiative to allow every student to have access to a device. We plan to nurture a generation of 21st-century learners with the skills and dispositions they need to be college and career ready. All of our students will feel like valued, respected members of the community, and student engagement will improve by 30 percent, as measured by an annual survey.

Your score: ______________________________

Why?

____

____

____

____

____

____

Draft your plan

Articulate your SMART goals

Now it's your turn. For each problem statement you have crafted, state your SMART goal. Be sure to provide metrics that show where you are now and where you are aiming to be each year. Remember, if you are choosing more than one problem to focus on, such as one core problem and one nonconsumption problem, name each initiative as Project 1, Project 2, and so forth, and write a separate SMART goal for each project.

Use the blank sheets at the end of the workbook if you need more space.

Before moving on, remember to self-assess your work. Look at the SMART Goals Rubric and see how you'd score yourself. Make any adjustments as necessary.

APPENDIX

Check for understanding: Avoid the technology trap

The following is the problem statement that focuses the most on student or school outcomes:

7—English language learners enter ninth grade two grade levels behind in math.

This is the most helpful problem statement, from a planning perspective, because all of the other problem statements focus on gaps in technology, not on outcomes.

Reflection question:

When planning teams begin by pinpointing learning goals, rather than by identifying technology gaps, they have the advantage of seeing the end from the beginning. Before committing a dollar, they are clear on their purpose. This perspective brings clarity to the design and planning phase. It helps the planning team imagine the changes that need to take place in the daily lives of students and teachers to bring about their goals. Then, after the design work is done, the planners are ready to make tactical decisions about which devices, software, and systems to install.

Practice evaluating: Score these problem statements

Problem statement 1

Our score: 3

Why? This team provides up-front data to support the argument that eighth-grade completion of Algebra I, combined with nurturing the mindset of agency, are critical to success to and through college. It provides baseline data to show where its students are now, and it justifies why those numbers are lower than they should be. The team provides a persuasive explanation of why it wants to redesign Algebra I and of the academic barriers that need to change.

Problem statement 2

Our score: 2

Why? On the positive side, the initial context and baseline data of this plan are helpful, and the team does not blame its problems on a lack of technology. To improve, the statement needs to go deeper in explaining the causal factors for the lagging achievement. Although the plan goes into some detail about low test scores, those are more evidence of problems than the problem itself. In its concluding sentence, the team names "empowerment" as a critical need, but it could go further to explain its theory about why a lack of empowerment is slowing down academic momentum and what the baseline metric is to quantify how bad the problem of lack of empowerment is.

Problem statement 3

Our score: 0

Why? This team makes the classic error of stating that they need technology because they do not have access to technology. Although they do provide a few baseline metrics, the data is used to justify more devices and professional development on how to use the technology and on how to do blended learning. This problem statement would be stronger if it discussed *why* blended learning is necessary in the first place. What barriers and gaps are there in the program that are preventing student achievement? Keep the focus on the students, not the technology.

Practice evaluating: Score these SMART goals

Statement 1

Our score: 3

Why? This district wants more of its graduates to graduate from college. The team turned that into a specific, actionable goal by aiming to get a number of students through Algebra I in eighth grade. Without being able to measure college completion rates yet, it developed proxy metrics to estimate whether its students are on track to graduate from college. If those proxy metrics are accurate, then the team has a way to check that its investment in Algebra I and student agency is paying off. The team looked at both academic and nonacademic outcomes by stating its goals related to student agency. The metrics are specific, include baselines, and show scale over time.

Statement 2

Our score: 2

Why? This SMART goal includes four metrics related to quantifiable increases over time in P-SAT scores, postsecondary readiness, and summative reading scores. Without baseline scores, however, it's hard to know whether the goals could be sequenced in a more realistic way—both to allow for an initial learning curve on everyone's part and to be appropriately ambitious over the entire four years. In addition, to depend on summative, end-of-year tests can be dangerous. Some schools find more success in identifying narrower goals related to knocking down learning barriers and improving skills, rather than waiting for a large, imprecise test to measure whether the program is working.

Statement 3

Our score: 1

Why? This goal focuses on technology for technology's sake. One of its key metrics is the ratio of devices to students ("1:1"), which says nothing about the more important question of student outcomes. The SMART goal would be stronger if the team were to center it around improving outcomes for students by removing learning barriers, not around equipping them with devices. Also, the goal lacks specificity. What does it mean to "nurture a generation of 21st-century learners," and how will the team measure that? What is "student engagement," and how will that be measured? Finally, the team should specify its goals sequentially to show how they broaden and deepen over three years.

Organize to Innovate

Key objectives

- Understand the different types of teams and what type of problem each can solve
- Pick the right team for your circumstances
- Select the right team members

Content summary

Getting the team right

After you have your SMART goals in place, the next step is to organize the right team to lead each project.

Giving teachers full autonomy to solve problems within their classrooms is important for solving some types of problems, but that approach also has its limits when teachers cannot change certain school architectures or district processes. By the same token, for teachers and schools just looking to get started on the road toward student-centered learning, there are many concrete and immediate steps an individual teacher can take to enhance her classroom on her own, without a school- or district-wide team. The trick is to diagnose the desired level of change, which then determines what type of team is necessary and ultimately who needs to be at the table.

Fundamentally, there are four different types of teams: functional, lightweight, heavyweight, and autonomous.

Functional teams, in which people work solely with others from their classroom or department, are best suited to improving one component of a service or one step of a process. Schools should use functional teams, made up of teachers or staff within the same department, to make changes that are not interdependent with other parts of the school.

Lightweight teams work well when a group decides to make improvements that affect how another group needs to do its job and when the relationship between the groups is predictable. A coordinative or project manager shuttles back and forth between groups working on a task to ensure that their work fits together correctly. Schools should use lightweight teams to coordinate projects that implicate more than one set of teachers, but in predictable ways.

Heavyweight teams are the best fit for those tasks requiring that both an organization's components and the people responsible for them interact with one another in new ways that cannot be anticipated or specified in advance; in other words, the problem requires a new system architecture. A heavyweight team comprises members from a variety of groups in an organization who bring their expertise, but not their loyalty to "how things have always been done." One person with significant clout who has the authority to make decisions leads the team. Schools should use heavyweight teams to implement sustaining innovations that require a fundamental redesign of how classrooms and departments interact.

Autonomous teams are essential for solving nonconsumption problems and creating disruptive innovations. They allow innovators to step outside of the existing context—including staffing, budget, facilities, and curriculum—to pioneer a new model based on a benefit such as personalization, access, or cost control. Schools should use autonomous teams when they want to do away with the factory-based classroom completely and replace it with a disruptive blended-learning model.

Check for understanding

Match the team to the task

To cement your understanding of the types of teams and which teams are the right match for different types of problems, draw lines below to connect each scenario in the first column to the type of team in the second column that is the best match for it. The answers are in the appendix at the end of this module.

Scenario	Type of team
1. A school wants to offer advanced and AP classes that it has not been able to in the past.	a. **Functional team** made up of teachers within the department.
2. Biology teachers want to create more time in class to do labs.	b. **Lightweight team** with a manager who shuttles back and forth between the various groups to coordinate.
3. Fifth-grade teachers want to create time in the day for students to improve their math skills by personalizing their learning, but the only computers in the school are in the school's computer labs, not in the classrooms.	c. **Heavyweight team** whose members colocate, leave behind their departmental interests, and have a senior manager with significant authority at the helm.
4. A school wants to improve students' literacy through a content-rich approach that relies on using all subject-matter teachers across the school.	d. **Autonomous team** with authority to redesign budget, staffing plans, curriculum, and facilities.

Content summary

How to pick the right type of team

The next step is to pick the right team to match the type of change you anticipate making. As you do so, you do not need to know what model of blended learning you want to deploy or what the design of the program will be. Each team you work with will collectively help design the right learning model to solve the appropriate SMART goal. But you do need to have a sense of the scope of the change that you want to realize.

To help gain a sense of the scope of change that you want to make, consider each SMART goal you have. The easy one to figure out is a SMART goal that tackles a nonconsumption problem. As we've discussed, if you're targeting nonconsumption, that means creating a disruptive learning experience relative to the traditional classroom. And that means you need an autonomous team.

For your SMART goals that represent a core problem, you have to dig a bit deeper to understand what type of team is likely to be the right match.

If your SMART goal is focused on a specific subject, grade level, or department, for example, that could signal that a functional team is the right fit. A classic example might be that English teachers want to create more time for them to give students richer feedback on writing assignments. But it could be the case that, for example, the best way to improve sixth-grade students' literacy is by tackling content knowledge and writing across the full curriculum in a coherent, coordinated, and iterative way, not just in an English class. This theory of action might suggest that a heavyweight team would be best.

Sometimes the answer will be clear to you from the SMART goal, but what should you do if the answer seems unclear?

The reality is that there are often multiple ways to solve problems. Although some solutions may produce better results than others in the ideal, they may also not be realistic in your particular circumstance. What's key is to take your SMART goal and combine it with the information from the Interest and Readiness Survey in Module 1.3 to understand your situation and the appetite for creating a school-wide solution (likely requiring a heavyweight team) versus one that cuts across some limited set of departments (likely requiring a lightweight team) versus one that resides within individual classrooms or one department (where a functional team will be best). In particular, pay attention to your answers to questions 1, 3, 4, 5, 6, 9, 13, and 20. These will help you determine what teams are even possible in your circumstance and help you select the right team for the level of change you have the desire and capacity to effect.

View rubric and benchmarks

Selecting the type of team

For each SMART goal you are addressing, you will write down the type of team you will use to tackle it. Then you will explain why that team is the right fit.

The Team Selection Rubric distinguishes an inadequate team selection (0) from one that is basic (1), advanced (2), and exceptional (3).

Team Selection Rubric

Exceptional 3	Advanced 2	Basic 1	Inadequate 0
Matches the **optimal type of team** to the scope of each task for each SMART goal and explains why this is a viable match.	Proposes a type of team that will work for the scope of each task for each SMART goal, but, based on the theory of what team is best for what type of problem, **a better option is available.**	Makes an effort to identify a team, but overall **misapplies the theory**.	Does not select a team or **does not use the theory** to explain why the choice was made.

Read through the following sample response to the prompt, followed by our evaluation of that selection according to the rubric. The example, developed by a real school team, has been modified slightly to retain its anonymity.

Sample team selection

We need an **autonomous** team to achieve our SMART goal because our plan incorporates major changes to the physical space in our building, the method of instruction, Wi-Fi capability, and our professional development. We must have an implementation team evaluate progress and make adjustments to ensure success. The components of our plan involve not only campus personnel but also district personnel in a joint effort to improve student performance and increase retention.

Scoring explanation

This is a strong statement that we would grade as advanced (2 points). Because the SMART goals of this district involve significant changes to and a redesign of the budget, staffing plans, curriculum, and facilities, the answer states clearly that an autonomous team with authority and stakeholder support is required for success. It is possible, however, that a heavyweight team would also be able to effect the changes this school seeks. A stronger statement would show why autonomy itself was critical and why this could not just be handled by a heavyweight team. It could do this by stating clearly that this was a nonconsumption problem, for example, and showcasing how critical it was to create wholly new processes and priorities outside of those of the traditional classroom.

Practice evaluating

Score these team selections

Rate the following team selections on a 0–3 scale (0 = inadequate, 1 = basic, 2 = advanced, 3 = exceptional) using the Team Selection Rubric. Explain your reasons why. Our answers are in the appendix at the end of this module.

Statement 1

Reimagining classrooms and reaching beyond grade-level boundaries will require our district to employ a **heavyweight** team for our blended-learning initiative.

To achieve our SMART goal, we must undertake significant changes on each campus. Teachers must have autonomy to alter current and acceptable policies of lesson planning and to change grading policies. Rather than submitting formal, specific lesson plans for each day, teachers in blended-learning classrooms must be allowed to think more in terms of longer-term and unit goals. To achieve their goals, teachers must be able to alter plans for the day at a moment's notice. Students will be progressing and reaching competencies at varying times, and teachers will respond to the needs of the students accordingly.

Additionally, our district's current policies of grading are a poor match for our blended-learning classrooms. Teachers will work collaboratively with district curriculum and instruction staff to create logical grading guidelines for their classrooms. We have begun serious discussions, at the request of the classroom teachers on the team, to alter bell schedules to allow for extended instructional time. These difficult and far-reaching changes for each campus reinforce our need for a heavyweight team for our blended-learning initiative. As additional phases of the initiative undergo planning and then begin, other classrooms and different grade levels will face the same sort of challenges. Creating empowered, heavyweight teams for these phases will be necessary to ensure they have the authority to make needed changes.

Your score: ______________________________

Why?

____

____

____

____

Statement 2

To achieve my SMART goal of increasing the amount of time I have to give my high school English students rich feedback on writing assignments so that they can bolster their writing abilities, I am using a **functional** team. I need to use time differently in my classroom, so I can tackle this problem by myself with perhaps the help of some peers within the English department who can help me with finding online resources. I don't think we will need outside assistance, although we will potentially need help procuring computers for during class time depending on our ultimate design. I also don't know if I'll need to coordinate with anyone to secure a writing aide for assistance.

Your score: ______________________________

Why?

____

____

____

____

Statement 3

To accomplish our SMART goal, our district's blended-learning program requires one district-level **autonomous** team and a **heavyweight** team on each pilot campus. The blended-learning program aims to improve students' capacity for lifelong learning and to increase reading scores through the implementation of a solution that moves us toward competency-based learning and away from the traditional seat-time based system. Implementing this type of system will require fundamental changes in class schedules, grading policies, staffing models, professional development, and curriculum design, necessitating the involvement of district officials with significant decision-making authority as well as others with formal leadership roles at both the school and district levels.

The heavyweight teams will include the teachers who are participating in the personalized-learning pilot as well as school leaders and instructional support staff. Heavyweight teams will be necessary at each campus as implementation begins and progresses throughout each school year in order to address various situations that develop. Campuses will be given the autonomy to make decisions as small as selecting new furniture to as large as redesigning class schedules that best fit their campuses' needs while supporting the district's overall vision.

Your score: ______________________________

Why?

____

____

____

____

Statement 4

To strengthen the transition from elementary to middle school (where students have much more autonomy than in our current model for elementary schools), our district wants to create fifth-grade classrooms within and across the district that switch from our traditional teacher-centered structure to flipped classrooms. In order to empower our fifth-grade teachers across all five of our elementary schools, we will leverage the **functional** teams in each school made up of every fifth-grade teacher. Working together, they can share ideas and best practices, then autonomously implement in their classrooms the flipped model that will enable their students to prepare to succeed in middle school.

Your score: ______________________________

Why?

____

____

____

____

Draft your plan

Select your type of team

Now it's your turn. Restate your SMART goal and then indicate which type of team you plan to organize to achieve the goal. Why is that the right team for the task?

SMART goal: ______________________________

Team type: ______________________________

Explain why this team is the right fit:

____

____

____

____

SMART goal: ______________________________

Team type: ______________________________

Explain why this team is the right fit:

____

____

____

____

If you plan to tackle more than two SMART goals, use the blank sheets at the end of the workbook to identify the right team for each project.

Before moving on, remember to self-assess your work. Look at the Team Selection Rubric and see how you'd score yourself. Make any adjustments as necessary.

Content summary

How to select team members

With the type of team picked, the next step is to figure out who should serve on the team. Consider choosing people who bring valuable expertise and skills, can help move things forward in the school, have launched initiatives in the past, or can block your plan if they don't approve of the ultimate design. Think outside the box as well. Team members can include parents, students, and community members in addition to the faculty and staff in the building and district if such selections make sense within the team structure.

If you are using a heavyweight or autonomous team, remember that you will need to appoint a senior leader with decision-making authority to oversee the team. If you are creating a lightweight team, you need a project manager who can shuttle between groups and help coordinate.

For each team, list the people who will serve on it and explain why those people are the right fit. Avoid naming more than one team for each problem. Of course, your main team may need to hand off some of the work to subordinate teams or committees, but for now, focus on the main team that will lead the effort. Usually these teams range from three to ten members. Next, if you are using an autonomous, heavyweight, or lightweight team, circle the name of the person who will be the leader or manager of the team and explain why she is ideal for this role. As a general rule, we've found that for the plan to be successful, the project leader or manager must be able to devote at least 50 percent of her time to developing and implementing the blended-learning plan.

View rubric and benchmarks

Selecting team members and a project manager

The following Team Member Selection Rubric distinguishes inadequate team member selections (0) from basic (1), advanced (2), and exceptional (3).

Team Member Selection Rubric

	Exceptional 3	Advanced 2	Basic 1	Inadequate 0
Team member selection	Thoughtful selection of members with **good reasons for each one**, based on the following requirements. *Requirements:* • Range of roles and individual selection matches the range of experiences needed to execute on SMART goal. • Team brings valuable skills, proper authority, and relevant experience. • Takes into account stakeholders who have the authority to block an initiative. • The number of individuals on the team matches the range of roles; there are not too many or too few people on the team. • Integrates community members beyond employees (e.g., parents, students, etc.), as appropriate.	Rationale for selection of members **meets most requirements**.	Rationale for selection of members **meets few requirements**.	There is **no rationale for selection of members OR** composition does not correspond to a specific type of team.

	Exceptional 3	Advanced 2	Basic 1	Inadequate 0
Project manager	Identifies a **qualified** manager who will oversee implementation; **describes the previous track record and time that the leader can devote to the project.**	Identifies a qualified manager, but **description leaves some questions** about the manager's track record and/or time the manager can devote to the project.	Identifies a qualified manager, but the **description is very incomplete or misguided.**	Does not identify a clear manager of the team, **OR** the description does not give any evidence of the manager being able to handle the role.

Read the following team member and project manager selection plan that a real school team developed and consider how you would score this example according to the preceding rubric. Compare your score to our analysis, which follows the example.

Sample team member and project manager selection

The autonomous team for implementation includes:

The school's principal—Critical to shuttle and coordinate between campus and district staff. Has also successfully piloted prior initiatives.

Instructional Media Specialist—Has expertise in instructional technology and has led teachers in our district and elsewhere through blended-learning pilots before.

Dean of Instruction—Has extensive experience guiding campuses to address student needs through instructional change.

Asst. Supt. of School Improvement—Has extensive experience guiding campuses to transform and address student needs.

Asst. Supt. of Finance—Critical for overseeing funding and technology purchases and other grants.

Chief Technology Officer—Critical for overseeing technology purchases.

Asst. Supt. for Facilities—Important for overseeing construction plans to renovate school using funds to accommodate Flex model for middle school students.

School Board Vice President—Promotes our blended-learning initiative in the community as well as with school board members to maintain school board support.

Director of Community and Parent Involvement—Assists with bilingual parent communication regarding blended learning and assists in fielding questions from parents about how blended learning will impact their child.

Our Instructional Media Specialist will serve as the director for this work. She has been in an instructional technology role for 12 years and is well known in our district as the person who pilots new instructional technology methods. She is capable of inspiring and motivating all teachers to see the power that blended learning will bring into their classrooms to differentiate instruction, provide personalized learning opportunities, increase student ownership, improve student performance through mastery-based learning, build relational capacity between students and staff, and prepare our students for high school. Our specialist has piloted and implemented multiple technology applications at the campus and district levels. She has also opened several new schools and established effective norms and expectations for instructional technology integration. Our specialist has written and facilitated face-to-face and online district technology professional development sessions for teacher reflection and growth.

Scoring explanation

We rate this answer as exceptional (6 points). This school has thoughtfully selected a right-sized set of team members with good reasons for each one. The team members match the range of experiences needed for the school to execute its SMART goal. The proposed team brings valuable skills, proper authority, and relevant experience to the blended-learning initiative, and it takes into account stakeholders who might block the plan's progress or who might not work for the school or system as is appropriate for the team structure. The school has thoughtfully selected its ideal project manager and provides a thorough description of a capable leader who is able to guide the district through its transition.

Practice evaluating

Team member and project manager selection

Rate the following team member selections on a 0–3 scale (0 = inadequate, 1 = basic, 2 = advanced, 3 = exceptional) using the Team Selection Rubric. Explain your reasons why. Our answers are in the appendix at the end of this module.

Practice statement

Our heavyweight team will comprise:

Superintendent—Respected leader who will have the necessary gravitas and respect from all parties to be the face of blended learning across our seven implementing schools and in the community.

Learning resource director—Varied background in education as a teacher and an administrator, both in K–12 and in higher education, makes him uniquely qualified to lead this project. Has led a complete program redesign in math and has served on state boards as an advisor for developmental education/career readiness. Has experience supervising large budgets, projects, and staff.

Seven school principals—Given the work required in each school, having school leader of each is critical.

All lead pilot teachers—All the lead teachers who are implementing the pilot will serve on the team to provide critical expertise in what will work with their students in the design and delivery of the initiative.

Because our blended-learning initiative involves two grade levels across seven schools, we need a project director who can coordinate across campuses and juggle multiple responsibilities. The learning resource director's vast experiences and ability to sit astride the district make him the perfect person to lead the team.

Your score: ______________________

Why?

____

____

____

____

____

____

Draft your plan

Identify your team members and project manager

Now it's your turn. List each team member whom you will recruit to lead your blended-learning initiative, what her role is in the school community, and why this person is right for the team. Pay attention to what role each team member will play on your functional, lightweight, heavyweight, or autonomous team.

Name: ______________________________

Role: ______________________________

Why on the team?

____

____

____

Name: ______________________________

Role: ______________________________

Why on the team?

____

____

____

Name: ______________________________

Role: ______________________________

Why on the team?

____

____

____

Name: ______________________________

Role: ______________________________

Why on the team?

____

____

____

Name: ______________________

Role: ______________________

Why on the team?

____

____

____

Name: ______________________

Role: ______________________

Why on the team?

____

____

____

Name: ______________________

Role: ______________________

Why on the team?

____

____

____

Name: ______________________

Role: ______________________

Why on the team?

____

____

____

Now circle the team member who will be the project leader or manager. Describe why this person is an ideal fit:

____

____

____

Repeat these steps for each problem and SMART goal you are addressing.

Before moving on, remember to self-assess your work. Look at the Team Member Selection Rubric and see how you'd score yourself. Make any adjustments as necessary.

As you work through the book, you may learn that you need more people involved to get your design right or to correctly implement it. If at any time you realize this, you can of course alter your team design—and in Part 3 of the book, we'll give you the dedicated space to reconsider the right type of team or who needs to be involved.

For now, next up is to sketch out the ideal student experience (Module 2.3).

APPENDIX

Check for understanding: Match the team to the task

1. d.
2. a.
3. b.
4. c.

Our evaluation of team selections

Statement 1

Our score: 3

Why? If the classrooms involved in this blended-learning initiative were one grade or subject level, a lightweight team might suffice in coordinating the autonomous efforts of individual teachers within individual classrooms to achieve their SMART goals. But because the proposed changes extend across grade levels and campuses within the district and appear to challenge some important policies in the district and potentially make changes to schedules within schools, a heavyweight team with decision-making authority is a sound choice. The district has offered a strong explanation of its reasons for that choice as well.

Statement 2

Our score: 2

Why? The teacher may be right that a functional team will allow her to accomplish her goals. Flipping the classroom, for example, could be an entirely adequate ultimate solution that might not require assistance outside of her classroom and department. There are some clues, however, that she should have at least considered using a lightweight team, as she indicates she may need help procuring computers for classroom time and coordinating with at least one outside writing aide. Although she may not need a lightweight team to facilitate this, coordinating across departments is the province of a lightweight team, so she should at least consider it and be clear about why one approach is better than the other. Had she chosen a lightweight team, she could have potentially assumed the role of teacher leader and been the project manager, marshaled support, built her own team, and coordinated across other departments to achieve her objectives.

Statement 3

Our score: 2

Why? The district correctly identifies that the level of change it is proposing will need *either* an autonomous team *or* a heavyweight team, but it does not need both. That will burden the project by creating far too much overhead. The fundamental changes it is proposing, however, do necessitate having a team with the level of clout that either a heavyweight or autonomous team would need.

Instead of having two teams, the district could create task forces as needed to address particular concerns or needs within content areas or on individual campuses as the program develops. As the plan rightly states, the team should include stakeholders from across the district.

Statement 4

Our score: 1

Why? Although the team is clearly identified and there is a clear rationale for the choice, the proposed change requires too much coordination across schools and across fifth-grade teams. Therefore, a lightweight team would be a better choice.

Our evaluation of team member and project manager selections

Our score: 6

Why? The district lists all of the team members who need to be on the heavyweight team and gives careful attention to having not just the direct and functional expertise on the team but also the superintendent, who will have the relational and political skills to handle all aspects of change within the community. The scope of team members appears likely to be correct. Finally, the plan presents a strong and succinct explanation for why the district chose the project director that it did.

Motivate the Students

Key objectives

- Identify your students' jobs to be done
- Articulate the experiences students need in order to satisfy their jobs
- Determine what you must provide and how, so that students will enjoy those experiences
- Design an idealized experience for students based on this work, one that will motivate them and help you accomplish your SMART goal

Content summary

Why motivation matters

With a rallying cry in mind and the right team assembled, you are ready to start designing your blended-learning solution. Ultimately, that solution will have many dimensions, including a strategy for staffing, devices, content, facilities, model selection, and culture. But the starting point for design, before any of these considerations, is to crawl inside the heads of students and look at school through their eyes.

When schools get the design right from the students' perspective, so that students feel that school aligns well with the things that matter to them, they show up to school motivated and eager to learn. By contrast, when teams design school without regard to the students' perspective, they face resistance at every turn from the very people they are trying to serve.

The first task for blended-learning teams, therefore, is to understand the student perspective and to design with student motivation as a guiding star.

Understanding the jobs-to-be-done theory in education

Schools are not alone in struggling to design an offering that their end users will willingly show up to devour. Companies struggle so desperately to predict whether a customer in a given demographic category will buy a new product because from the customer's perspective, the market is not structured by customer or product category.

Instead, people have *jobs to be done* in their lives—*the progress that they are trying to make in a particular circumstance.* Understanding the job helps us understand *why* people do the things they do and what their underlying motivation is. Every job has functional, social, and emotional dimensions to it; oftentimes the social and emotional dimensions of a job are more important to understand than the functional ones.

A job is critically different from the traditional marketing concept of "needs." Needs always exist in someone's life, but they fail to capture what someone is prioritizing in a particular circumstance and thus what will motivate the person to take action.

Just as many people deprioritize the job of "maintain my physical health"—even though it is something they *should* pay attention to and *need* to do—many students languish in school or do not come to class at all because education isn't a job that they are trying to do. Education is something they might choose to *hire* to do that job—but education itself isn't the job. This distinction between thinking about a student's needs and what they are in fact motivated to do separates the jobs-to-be-done theory from other research about students' developmental "needs" based on their age or other such milestone. Teachers can work extraordinarily hard to improve the features of their products, in the hope that more engaging lessons, media, and student-response clickers will improve student motivation. But their efforts are in vain if they are aimed at providing an even better way for students to do something that they were never trying to do in the first place.

This is not to say that a school should not instill in students certain core knowledge, skills, and dispositions to prepare them to fulfill their potential and be thriving citizens; rather, that in order to accomplish these objectives, the school must create an experience that is intrinsically motivating for students. School can be a place where students find joy in learning. The key is to crawl into the learners' skin and see their circumstances—including their anxieties, immediate problems, and innate motivations—from their point of view.

At a high level and as recounted in depth in *Blended,* we have observed that there are two core jobs that most students have:

1. They want to feel successful—that they are making progress and accomplishing something, rather than experiencing nothing but repeated failure or running up against walls.

2. They want to have fun with friends. They want positive, rewarding social experiences with others, including peers, teachers, coaches, advisors, and other potential friends.

As a result, schools are in competition with such activities as gang membership, dropping out of school to take a job or hang out with friends, playing video games, playing pickup basketball, and any number of other nonacademic options as something that students can hire to experience success and have fun with friends. Too often, schools are sorry competitors for these alternatives, as factory-model schools don't allow most students the opportunity to experience success or have fun with friends in the course of their work. Students who do not hire school to do their job but instead focus their attention on things besides education are not unmotivated. They are plenty motivated—to feel success and have fun with friends. The problem is that a surprising number of students just don't or can't feel successful each day and find rewarding relationships at school. Instead, school makes them feel like failures—academically, socially, or both.

Students of course have many other jobs that arise constantly. Identifying the jobs that students in your school have—and then designing to get them done—is critical.

Check for understanding

Understanding a student's motivation

Circle the statements that are correct. The answers are in the appendix at the end of the module.

A job to be done . . .

1. Is ever-present in someone's life regardless of circumstance.
2. Has emotional and social dimensions to it as well as functional ones.
3. Is the same as someone's needs.
4. Refers to the progress someone is trying to make in a particular circumstance.
5. Helps us design a service around a person's underlying motivation.

Reflection question

How can understanding a student's job to be done help you understand what a student *will* do, not what she perhaps *should* do?

____

____

____

Content summary

Identifying students' jobs to be done

How do you identify the jobs that your particular students have in their lives, beyond the two we have identified? Directly asking students will rarely work. People generally can't articulate their jobs to be done in a straightforward way. Listening to their own explanations of their motivations will typically mislead you, as they describe what they think you want them to say or misunderstand the myriad of forces acting on their own decision making.

Instead, the key is to spot areas where students are frustrated or confronting barriers to their making progress. There are many ways of unearthing these moments. Here are six of our favorites:

1. Interview individual students to create a mini-documentary—or narrative—of the moments leading up to an action a student took or a decision a student made, so that you can understand the student's true motivation and the trade-offs she is willing to make.

2. Recall a time when you solved a frustrating problem for an individual student in your class or helped her make progress on something where she was struggling—and the student showed visible relief and significant gratitude.

3. Observe the times during the school day or year when students can't find any solution that satisfies their job and they opt to do nothing instead.

4. Shadow a student for a day and observe all the workarounds and compensating behaviors she exhibits.

5. Look for what students don't want to do.

6. Notice when, to get their work done, students use the classroom materials, school's facilities, or teachers and staff in unusual ways that depart from conventional wisdom. Chances

are, these alternative uses are telling you something about a job they have.

Three levels in the architecture of a job

There are three levels in the architecture of a job. At the foundational level is the job itself. The second level is composed of all the experiences that you have to provide to get the job done perfectly. Once you understand all those experiences, you can implement the third level: properly integrating the right assets together to provide each of the experiences necessary to do the job perfectly.

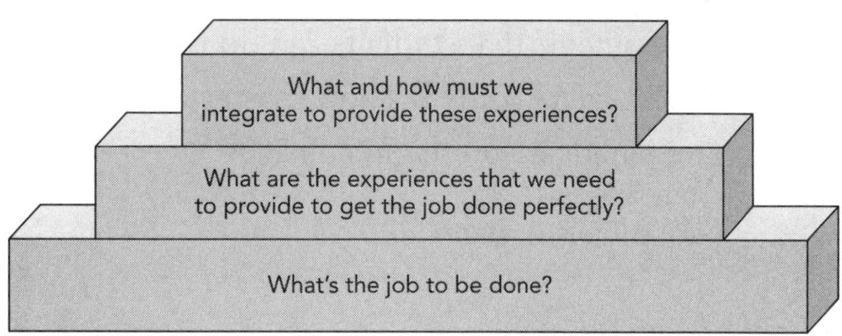

Brainstorming and detailing the experiences that make up the second level of a job can be challenging. Individuals and teams tend to spend a long time really delving into the experiences needed to deliver on a student's job. For illustrative purposes, here are ten experiences you might consider:

Access to actionable data and rapid feedback

Health and wellness services

Mastery or competency-based learning

Meaningful work experiences

Mentoring experiences

Physical exercise

Positive group experiences

Quiet reading time

Student agency

Transparency in learning goals

After determining the experiences that you have to provide to get the job done perfectly, move to the third level of the job by identifying what resources you must have and how you must knit them together to deliver the intended experiences. For example, you might decide that having adaptive learning software is critical for students to experience individual mastery. You might also—or instead—decide that it is critical to have valid, short oral assessments that students can do with a teacher whenever they feel they are ready to show mastery. For illustrative purposes, here are ten ideas you might consider:

Adaptive software

Apprenticeships

Career certifications

Game-based learning

Expeditions

Individual tutoring and feedback

Learning badges

Personalized learning plans

Project-based learning

Socratic discussions

Apply the learning

Design using the jobs-to-be done theory

Getting the design right from the students' perspective is the key to improving student engagement. Now it's your turn to design using the jobs-to-be-done theory as your guide. Let's work on the three levels in the architecture of a job, taking them one at a time.

Brainstorm students' jobs

Referring to the primary problems you identified in the Rallying Cry module (2.1), reflect on the different unmet jobs students have that may be contributing to those problems. List here the students' jobs that, if addressed, would help you achieve your SMART goals. We've started you off with the two high-level jobs that we have identified. For each job, frame it from the students' perspective—"Help me . . ."—so that you are truly seeing the world through their eyes and thinking about their motivations. Be sure to think through the functional, social, and emotional dimensions. We provide room for ten jobs; once you have identified three to five jobs per SMART goal, you have more than enough to get going.

1. Help me feel successful
2. Help me have fun with friends
3. Help me . . . ______________________________
4. Help me . . . ______________________________
5. Help me . . . ______________________________
6. Help me . . . ______________________________
7. Help me . . . ______________________________
8. Help me . . . ______________________________
9. Help me . . . ______________________________
10. Help me . . . ______________________________

Identify necessary experiences

For each of the jobs you identified, use the Getting the Jobs Done chart here to detail the experiences you would want to provide to get those jobs done successfully. For example, mastery or competency-based learning may be a key experience for students to feel successful—such that students should be able to make progress as quickly or slowly as they are able to demonstrate their preparedness to move on, and that each student's pace should be individual, not collective. Inherent in this concept is that students work within their zone of proximal development on skills that are "just above" their own current capabilities: not too difficult and not too easy, with occasional opportunities to stretch or challenge themselves.

For now, ignore the fourth column ("What to integrate and how") on the Getting the Jobs Done chart. We'll tackle that later. Focus on the student experiences.

Getting the Jobs Done

Job	SMART Goal	What experiences do students need?	What to integrate and how
Example 1: Help me feel successful	[Write your SMART goal here]	Student agency—empowering students to set individual learning goals and providing them with enough time to make progress toward them	Utilize PLP tool to give students access to a variety of curated learning resources organized by competency in a playlist, such that students can choose how they learn. Implement within learning cycle in which students set a goal, plan how they'll realize the goal, learn, show evidence of learning, reflect, and repeat.
Example 2: Help me have fun with friends	[Write your SMART goal here]	Meaningful work experiences in collaboration with peers, teachers, and community members, both in and out of school, but connected directly to the curriculum, learning goals	Project time each day for two hours, plus "expeditions" where students work off-campus in jobs, community organizations, etc., for two weeks, four times a year.

Decide what to integrate and how

Now consider the third level of the job: what resources to use and how to integrate them into your operations to deliver on the experiences that you brainstormed. For example, if you intend for students to experience agency, you might conclude that a student-driven software platform is a key resource that will be necessary to give students the choice and control that define a high-agency environment. You might also determine that you need to develop and implement a learning cycle in which students set a goal, plan how they'll realize the goal, learn, show evidence of learning, reflect, and repeat. Whatever you decide, list them in the fourth column in the Getting the Jobs Done chart. The more specific you are, the better.

Content summary

Creating day-in-the-life stories

The next step is to put these elements—specifically the items you identified in the "What to integrate and how" column—into a coherent vision for what the student experience will look like.

At this stage, we encourage designers to hold to a lofty vision unencumbered by the reality of their current school day or their current resources. As we work through this book, plenty of the future steps will tether designers back to reality, but at this stage, having a "blue sky" mentality—that is, opening up your mind as widely as possible—is critical so that you don't artificially constrain what is possible.

All too often, educators are told not to dream but just to focus on the here and now and what their current budget affords them. But dreaming big is important. As our friend Alex Hernandez, a partner at the Charter School Growth Fund, has said,

> We advise our school designers not to start with the school schedule when they advise schools. The reason is, blended learning is this big, open canvas, and what you do when you start with a schedule is you basically drop a thousand constraints [on that canvas]. You're giving away stuff that you're not even prepared [to give away], or have thought about giving away. And so where we do ask folks to start is, we say, "Start with the learning environment. And I don't care if it's thirty kids or it's ninety kids. And let's not think too much about the space at this point. Think about the experiences that you want students to have academically, socially. And, yeah, let's not do too many, but let's just think through, like, if we wanted to do three or four of these different experiences during a certain block of time." So you start putting boundaries around these experiences. How do you create these experiences for students? And that's the beginning of school design.

That describes exactly what we want to do with the jobs-based thinking. The first step now is to map out what a student will experience in your school or class that you are blending. Be forewarned that this is a first step and a first draft of that student experience. As we march forward in the book, we will consider new layers that will cause you to adjust that experience—for example, starting in Module 2.4, we'll think about the teacher's role. But it's healthy to think about the ideal student experience in a vacuum through the jobs-to-be-done lens first.

To that end, we'll start by writing out a day-in-the-life story of a hypothetical student.

View rubric and benchmarks

Articulating the student experience

To assist you in crafting a day-in the-life story, the following Student Experience Rubric distinguishes an inadequate student experience description (0) from one that is basic (1), advanced (2), and exceptional (3).

Student Experience Rubric

	Exceptional 3	Advanced 2	Basic 1	Inadequate 0
Design work	Designs a plan that **shows students' daily and weekly experiences** for each project from at least two perspectives; the plan includes **varied academic and social experiences**.	Provides a complete design, but it leaves **some question** about what the student experience will involve.	Provides a basic design, but it leaves **major questions** about what the student experience will involve.	Does not provide a tangible design beyond buzzwords.

	Exceptional 3	Advanced 2	Basic 1	Inadequate 0
Application of jobs-to-be-done theory	Designs a **comprehensive plan** that unlocks students' intrinsic motivations of feeling successful each day and having fun with friends while accounting for other barriers that require remediation (e.g., physical activity, work-related commitments).	Designs a plan that unlocks students' intrinsic motivations, but **does not account for other barriers**.	Designs a plan, but it **does not unlock students' intrinsic motivations**.	Does not present any compelling set of experiences.
Link	Provides a **fully reasonable rationale** for why the new student experience will mitigate the problem identified in Section 1: Rallying Cry.	Presents a **mostly** reasonable link between the design and the problem.	Presents a **somewhat** reasonable link between the design and the problem.	Does not connect the design to the problem.

Read through the following example of a story that a real school team developed, followed by our evaluation of that story according to the rubric.

Sample day-in-the-life story

Personalized Learning Time (PLT): Student choice and pace

During Personalized Learning Time, students access digital content and assessments within the PLP (Personalized Learning Plan) that address critical skills each student must acquire in each course, grade level, and unit of instruction. After students take a diagnostic assessment to assess their understanding of the content, they are able to select the content that best meets their preferred mode of learning and academic goals. Students move at their own pace throughout the content. Once they feel confident with the material, they request a content assessment that enables them to show mastery of content. Students must show 80 percent or higher mastery to move on to the next concepts. PLT is not solely about "screen time." Students will have the option to participate in teacher-led small-group instruction sessions known as workshops, student-led small-group sessions, or individualized peer-to-peer tutoring, as needed.

Project time

Students will work on real-world projects that are extensions of content-level learning objectives. Students will work independently and in groups to explore real-world problems and challenges in an active and engaging way. The intent is to inspire students to obtain a deeper understanding of the concepts they are learning while developing cognitive skills. Product creation and presentation are a large part of the grade. Projects are designed to be cross curricular; this ensures that reading and writing skills are heavily embedded in all projects. This supports our SMART goal of improving student reading scores in grades 3–12.

Mentor time between teachers and students

Mentees meet with their mentors for 10 minutes for their weekly check-in. Students drive these meetings to discuss their proposed goals and plans for the coming week and reflect together on the past week. The mentor helps students set goals, create plans, shift strategies when needed, and reflect on progress—the skills of becoming a self-directed learner. The mentor and family work together to support a student's goals and academic success.

Socratic seminars will be used to teach successful dialogue skills and develop "soft skills."

Reading Time is time during which students will be reading digital and traditional paper books. Students will read for a minimum of 30 minutes daily in a variety of ways such as silent reading, guided reading, group reading, and interactive grouping. Teachers will check in with students, read alongside them, and ask questions to check for comprehension. Reading Time is being incorporated to address the declining reading scores at grades 3–12.

Solving Time is dedicated time for students to work on math skills. Students will work in small, teacher-led groups designed to give students quick, targeted instruction and feedback, as needed. At all times, students will be provided with several different options and levels of support to ensure that they are always moving toward achieving their highest potential.

A day in the life of Miguel

Miguel is a high-achieving student, but he has been bored and disruptive in a traditional classroom. Our blended-learning program allows Miguel to use the Personalized Learning Plan (PLP) dashboard to excel through content at his own pace during PLT. He chooses the content that motivates him. Miguel is not held back by the structure of a traditional classroom; he has the option to complete Challenge Focus content areas in the PLP that are more advanced and provide him with content that is rigorous. As a result, he is no longer bored in class, and his behavior has improved. Miguel actively participates in collaborative project time and assists other students during PLT when needed. He is now exhibiting signs of a true leader while working with teams. Miguel meets with his mentor on Friday to set goals for the next exciting week. He no longer needs ongoing support from his teacher to stay focused and on task. He has developed habits of success that allow him to set goals, stay engaged, and shift strategies as needed.

A day in the life of Julia

Julia is a struggling student who has been identified as being at-risk. Math and reading are her most challenging subjects; her favorite subject is science. Julia has many academic foundational gaps, so she receives lots of support. She begins each week reviewing real-time data in her PLP with her mentor to set goals for the week and prioritize where she will spend her time. She reviews the online content during PLT as many times as she needs until she masters the content. On the whiteboard is a list of the workshops her teacher is offering today. She is glad to see that her teacher is offering a workshop on fractions. That's great because she didn't understand the fraction video she watched last night and needs more help. During Solving Time, Julia receives targeted one-on-one and small-group support from her teacher and sometimes Miguel. She also has the option to come in 30 minutes before school to attend "office hours," additional targeted instruction for Julia to ensure that she will master content. During daily Reading Time, it is evident that Julia is becoming a more confident reader; she is actively participating in Socratic seminars and reading more books. She has become more outgoing and offers peer support in science, her favorite subject.

Scoring explanation

We give this description a full 9 points. It is a clear and compelling plan for the student experience within this school's initiative, and it shows clearly what the students' lives will be like in the program with in-depth perspectives of two students at different places along the learning spectrum. Both students are better and more precisely served by the new model such that they have more opportunities to be successful each day. They can each envision, structure, and track their own academic progress, and the plan comprehensively details the many ways they can have fun with their friends, from Socratic discussions to collaborative projects to open lab time and peer mentoring. The plan also explains fully how the newly blended, personalized, and varied student experience will enable all students to reach their full potential and raise the overall reading and math levels across the school.

Practice evaluating

Day-in-the-life stories

Rate the following day-in-the-life stories on a 0–3 scale (0 = inadequate, 1 = basic, 2 = advanced, 3 = exceptional; maximum possible score = 9) using the Student Experience Rubric. Explain your reasons why. Our answers are in the appendix at the end of this module.

Statement 1

Sofia, a Hispanic fifth grader who is an English Language Learner (ELL) and low income, is not reading on grade level.

Day in the Life in Year 3 of the School

The day starts at 7:30 a.m. for the school-provided free breakfast. Sofia's morning routine includes brief socializing with her classmates and discussing the plans for the day. While in the school commons area, Sofia and her friends watch the live school announcements. The bell rings for the first curriculum block. They each log into their learning management system and receive their personalized schedule. Sofia and her friends compare schedules for the day. Sofia is scheduled to begin the block by meeting with her teacher for small-group instruction while one of her friends (who is reading above grade level) has a choice of where to begin.

8:00–8:45 Balanced Literacy

The teacher provides whole-group instruction on a new concept—nonfiction texts and time lines—and engages the students in a Socratic discussion of the concept. The teacher moves on to personalized instruction with small groups.

8:45–10:00 Morning Block

Sofia proceeds to small-group guided reading with her teacher. After a 20-minute session, Sofia has a quick conference with her teacher to discuss progress and to reflect on her work plan. They discuss what her schedule for this week will look like. Toward the end of the morning block, Sofia and her friends begin to work together on a project about the evolution of voting rights in the country. Sofia joins her friends to watch a video that the teacher created demonstrating the expectations for the project. They then go to suggested websites to begin research for the first assignment. When the bell rings, Sofia meets with the teacher again, who provides interventions for her reading module. (Sofia had been scoring low on the reading assessments and did not make sufficient progress on her interim assessment.)

10:00–10:30 Recess

10:30–11:30 Language Arts Intervention/Enrichment Block

During this block, Sofia will meet with an interventionist for support with her reading skills.

11:30–12:00 Lunch

12:00–1:15 Afternoon Block

The next instructional block, math/science, begins. Sofia checks her online personalized learning plan, which lists what she has completed and what is still pending, along with her weekly goal, and realizes that she has questions concerning her math content. She meets with her teacher for a mini-lesson that provides support based on her individual needs. She then begins her competency-based math lesson. After completing the online test, she receives her mastery score and immediate feedback indicating the areas in which she needs additional practice. Because she scored high enough to skip the lesson, the system moves on to the next module.

1:15–2:00 Math and Science Intervention/Enrichment Block

The teacher provides whole-group instruction on new concepts. The teacher then moves on to personalized instruction with small groups.

2:00–2:30 Math and Science Intervention/Enrichment Block (continued)

Sofia and her friends then meet up again during their enrichment block and start working on a different project based on an outside passion of theirs. The project allows both Sofia and her friends to explore their personal interests and is aligned to the state standards.

2:30–3:00 Recess (and Dismissal, for some students)

3:00–5:30 Extended Day

During the extended day, students have the ability to move among flexible groups, depending upon their needs. This is a variation of the Station Rotation model that allows students to fill learning gaps. They may seek assistance from their mentor teacher, from a peer, or through individual learning.

Your score: ______________________________

Why?

____

____

____

____

____

____

Statement 2

I'm gonna be honest with you. I did NOT want to come to this thing. Who wants to go to school in the summer? But given that I haven't even turned 11 yet, if I want to go anywhere, somebody has to drive me and usually that's my mom, so that means summer school for me. The thing is—and I know this is weird—but I feel like a little bit of a different person from who I was two weeks ago. Take directions, for example. In normal school in fifth grade, our teacher would give us directions for that period of what we had to finish. Sometimes I'd do it, but honestly, a lot of the time I just didn't see the point except to not be that guy to get in trouble (and at this point I'm kinda used to that so it doesn't matter much). But then at this boot camp, the schedule was all crazy—the entire time before lunch, I was going to be on my own and supposed to be this thing called self-directed. At first I was like, "No way! I have no idea what is going on." But in the morning I got to meet with the teacher I'm going to have next year for sixth-grade math, and he taught us how that means we set directions for ourselves. He taught us about how to really set a goal—not just say "I want to play ball at this college blah blah blah," but to make it something you can do as a step to that. For example, "By the end of today, I want to be able to find the area of a large pizza," and then make a plan to find what you need to learn to do that. It's pretty cool.

They have all these things about the math topics online, and you can either watch that by yourself, or ask a friend for help, or go meet with one of the teachers. For the first time ever I feel like I can see where we're going in school past just that day. It's like I've got a map for this summer school but also for the rest of the year and however fast or slow I want to get there, it's up to me. I want to go fast so that way I can start learning geometry because you get to build stuff. The other thing that's changed for me is what it means to be good at math. I used to think that was just for the kids who were always doing everything the teacher said and who got A's, not me. But every single day for the past two weeks, I've been good at math, and it's because I'm doing the steps I need to get me to my goal. I don't have to compare myself to anyone because we're all learning our own thing here and people are good in different ways, but as long as you're working toward what you need to learn, you can be good at math.

I have three favorite parts. The first is the cafeteria. It looks so different from the normal school year! We're using it as a space for our core skills. We can sit anywhere we want as long as we keep ourselves on-task. If I need extra help, I can go to a breakout corner with whatever teacher I want or go up to my friend and ask him. There's a really smart kid that sits near me, and he can always explain math in a way I understand. The teachers also have these areas set up if you want to learn through a project like I did with graphs. Sometimes, if I start doing something myself, the lesson makes way more sense.

The second thing I like is the afternoon. We get to work on projects and pick our own teams. My friends and I had this idea that we could graph the number of free throws each of us made over how many tries we took and then compare to see who had the highest percentage of made shots to tried shots.

My third favorite thing is that for the first time I can remember in school, I'm getting asked what I think. There's this person there who says she's my learning coach's coach (that's cool teachers can learn, too), and she asks me all the time what I thought about that lesson, and what I think could make learning that math skill better. I got to show her my favorite math game online, and she put it with the adding negatives lesson as something you can do to understand the video better, so that made me feel really good because now another kid can learn from what I think is fun.

Sample Schedule: Students will spend most of their day on their personally customizable flex pathway, moving on to new skills when they show mastery. For the Project-Based Learning Time, students will be in heterogeneous groups solving self-directed real-world problems using middle school math thinking. Teachers will act as mentors and coaches throughout the process and meet with their students each morning and afternoon to address concerns and accelerate learning.

Your score: ______________________________

Why?

____

____

____

____

____

____

Statement 3

Lucas is a student at our urban district's alternative high school, which is located across the highway from the largest high school in our district and next door to our county's health and human services center. Most of the students in our alternative high school have had interrupted academic experiences for a variety of reasons—pregnancy, juvenile detention, or behavioral problems. Our alternative high school doesn't have a traditional graduation date in June (or even December). Instead, we individualize all students' experiences through an Enriched Virtual model of blended learning, so that when students have completed their online coursework to fulfill their missing credits, they can receive their high school diplomas and move on to the work and family lives that many of them have already begun. The counselors at our school offer mandatory individual and group counseling sessions with our students, as well as life skills classes.

Although Lucas is 16 years old, his math competency is at the 7th-grade level. In addition to his other core curriculum requirements, he needs math credits through Algebra II to qualify for graduation. He would like to earn his high school diploma before he turns 19, but he will need to complete at least four years' worth of math within that time. Lucas does not have the support at home nor the out-of-school schedule to enable him to complete his online course work there, so all of his online academic work takes place at school in a computer lab setting.

Lucas is motivated, however, to graduate. His drug addiction rehabilitation while in detention built his persistence and ability to envision his future.

Your score: ______________________

Why?

____

____

____

____

____

____

Draft your plan

Write your day-in-the-life story

Now it's your turn to draft your own story.

For this exercise and the others in this chapter, draft the story for one of your SMART goals. For the other SMART goals you plan to tackle, use the blank sheets at the end of the workbook to draft these stories.

Day in the life of a hypothetical student

Before moving on, remember to self-assess your work. Look at the Student Experience Rubric and see how you'd score yourself.

Practice evaluating

Week-in-the-life story

Next up is to do the same thing, but this time for a week in the life of that same student. We've provided one example so that you can think about how a week-in-the-life story differs from a day-in-the-life one, and you can use the same Student Experience Rubric to grade it. Our answer is in the appendix.

Week-in-the-life story

A typical week in the life of a student in our district's blended-learning pilots throughout our elementary schools, where students range in age from 3 (preschool) to 11 (5th grade), will begin Monday morning when teachers help students set personalized-learning goals. Students will be able to see what competencies are up next in their weekly planner for each station.

Because all classrooms in our elementary schools are self-contained, we can create very flexible schedules that can be modified daily to meet the needs of the learners. Teachers can work with large blocks of time and allow students to choose when and how they work on any one competency—either with the guided instruction of their teacher, with software, in an offline activity, or with a small group. Teachers will help students set goals to at least keep pace with the suggested calendar to avoid falling behind and to maintain a set level of performance. Teachers will also provide students with feedback and discuss on Fridays what the progress data shows from the just-completed week.

Every elementary student's favorite time of the day, aside from lunch and recess, is center time. Blended learning taps into that immensely powerful and productive small-group time and connects it to meaningful activity that helps knowledge to stick in a learner's brain and connect that learning. That foundation of center time will be the central cog around which learning will run throughout our elementary schools. Creating groups of learners that are constantly changing throughout the day, based upon the competency and skill on which they are working, will keep learners invested and excited about learning and will make it fun for these learners, a requirement for productivity and retention. Working in groups and centers all day will also reduce or completely eliminate the need for students to be pulled out of class for remediation, thereby allowing them to remain with their classmates all day long.

Young learners are naturally curious, creative, and social. Our elementary schools will be a place where their curiosity and creativity can thrive. Even students this young will have some choice in their activities and assessments. Students will be able to demonstrate learning and mastery in a variety of ways, through products, presentations, and creative activities, and not only through paper-and-pencil assessments. Students will have more than one attempt to master the competencies, but again will have the opportunity for instruction in a different manner from previously used. The pressure and disempowerment that learners currently feel—which cause them to burst into tears, misbehave rather than admit they don't know, or fake a stomachache—will be a thing of the past as learners are met right where they are, at their level, and get to make their choices about learning while having fun with others and being creative. Instead of centers being a 60-minute block in the day, centers will be the majority of the day. Our students will thrive as a result.

Your score: ______________________________

Why?

____

____

____

____

____

____

Draft your plan

Write your week-in-the-life story

Now it's your turn to draft your own story.

Week in the life of a hypothetical student

Before moving on, remember to self-assess your work. Look at the Student Experience Rubric and see how you'd score yourself.

Now write another story for a different hypothetical student to show how the experiences differ.

Day in the life of a different hypothetical student

Week in the life of a different hypothetical student

Before moving on, remember to self-assess your work. Look at the Student Experience Rubric and see how you'd score yourself. Pay particular attention to how these two stories combine with the first stories you wrote to create a holistic design—and see how the stories hang together.

Next, explain how this new design will be an improvement compared to your old design in helping students fulfill the jobs they are trying to do in their lives. Being explicit about how the blue-sky design you have in mind will get these jobs done is critical to keep you on point. As you write this, if you want to go back and edit your earlier stories, feel free to do so. Throughout this process, iteration will be critical.

____

____

____

____

____

Why will this new design help solve the problem you are addressing and attain your SMART goal? If you want to rewrite your earlier stories as you think through this question, feel free to do so.

____

____

____

____

____

Repeat these steps for each problem and SMART goal you are addressing.

As we continue to work through this book, you will have to make modifications to what you just wrote. Perhaps the technology you want to use isn't available, or your school's staffing model won't enable you to let a student work with multiple teachers at once. That's OK. The rest of the book is designed to scaffold you through the design process so that you can make these trade-offs as needed—but at least you're starting with an ideal vision for what you want the student experience to be like to achieve your SMART goal.

APPENDIX

Check for understanding: Understanding a student's motivation

Statements 2, 4, and 5

Our evaluation of day-in-the-life stories

Statement 1

Our score: 8

Why? This school has designed an engaging plan that shows clearly what Sofia's life will be like in its blended-learning initiative. It offers a sense of how Sofia's classmates will move through the day as well, although there are questions as to whether all students can be accommodated in the plan, which is why we subtracted 1 point. The plan comprehensively details how Sofia will be motivated during every school day, from having a fun and productive time with her friends in the cafeteria during breakfast (where they are each actively planning their own days ahead of them) and continuing all the way through her extended day. The plan builds in multiple opportunities for Sofia to chart her academic successes. In creating this new student experience, the plan provides the structure and content that will help Sofia engage fully in her education and master the reading, writing, and math skills she needs to be successful in middle school and beyond.

Statement 2

Our score: 7

Why? This plan provides a *mostly complete design* of the student experience, but it raises a few questions about what the specifics of that will involve, especially relative to scheduling and assessment. The great strength of this plan is how compellingly it imagines and expresses the student's emotional, social, and intellectual experience (among both peers and adults) from his own perspective, although it does leave it a bit open as to how he will track his progress and feel successful in his academic work. The Flex model the summer school is employing here should provide students with the skills they need to succeed in middle school math in the fall, but the plan doesn't completely explain how the school will know whether this design has solved the problem of unpreparedness.

Statement 3

Our score: 3

Why? This plan provides a basic design of the school's blended-learning plan. Students independently do their core curriculum online and then meet with other students in counseling and life skills classes. The plan, however, leaves open major questions about how Lucas's or any other student's day actually unfolds, in terms of both the schedule and the lived experience for each student. Lucas's past experiences and his current goals and determination themselves are compelling, but this plan leaves unanswered a deeply concerning question relative to students' job of having fun with friends. It isn't clear that Lucas will have any time at school with other students, other than in the counselor-led mandatory therapy and life skills sessions. Finally, the Enriched Virtual model will give Lucas flexibility to proceed at his own pace through the academic material he needs to master for graduation, but as this plan is written, there isn't a clear explanation of how he can feel successful on a daily basis about what he is achieving, nor how he will plan (and access the support of both peer and adult mentors) to accomplish all that he needs to in the next two years.

Our evaluation of week-in-the-life story

Our score: 8

This example of students' experiences is just one part of a district's ambitious overall project, and it shows clearly in what ways these elementary students' lives will improve through the district's new blended-learning initiative. The plan reveals a compelling understanding of and compassion for the developmental needs and jobs to be done of the district's elementary students, and it illustrates a comprehensive Monday-through-Friday routine that allows each student to have fun throughout the days and in different ways with their friends, as well as to feel the satisfaction that comes from academic progress. The plan allows for varied types of assessment ("not only through pen-and-paper assessments"), which will expand students' sense of success. The plan provides a fully reasonable explanation for how problems of lagging student performance and high rates of tardiness and absenteeism will be mitigated by the blended-learning initiative. The plan could include more specifics that illustrate how an entire week will unfold for a learner and how activities—beyond goal setting—will or will not vary day to day. Therefore, we marked it down 1 point for its design work.

Elevate Teaching

Key objectives

- ○ Integrate teachers' roles to deliver the ideal student experience
- ○ List the key roles teachers will need to play in your design
- ○ Understand the difference between motivating and hygiene factors
- ○ Identify specific motivators that your blended-learning design seeks to amplify for teachers
- ○ Articulate strategies to amplify these motivators

Content summary

Teaching still matters—but will look different

With your ideal—and idealistic—school design in place for students, it's now time to think about the teachers and add another perspective to your design. As you consider the role of teachers (yes, for many reading this book, this is you!) and, in future chapters, technology, content, and the physical school building, your design will inevitably shift. But for now, the first place to start is in matching the teaching experience to your ideal student experience. Then we'll consider the world from the point of view of teachers and from the perspective of how best to use the teachers you have.

Intuition and a great deal of evidence tell us that good teachers have a lasting influence on student outcomes. It's no different in blended learning. In the good blended-learning programs we have observed, although the teacher role shifts in profound ways—teachers may no longer be doing lesson planning for and leading an entire class on the same activity—they are still engaged and working with students even more actively. In the bad blended-learning programs that we have observed, the teacher feels replaced and often sits in the back of the room, disgruntled and disengaged from the students, who in turn tend not to learn nearly as much as they might with an engaged, enthusiastic teacher.

As you design teachers' experiences to match the ideal student experience, we recommend keeping two things in mind.

Move beyond lockstep instruction

Top-down, teacher-centered, monolithic instruction is an uninspiring choice for creating the entrepreneurial, inquisitive problem solvers that today's employers are paying top dollar to recruit.

Even as many teachers across the United States have attempted to shed aspects of the lecture format over the last several decades, the factory-model classroom design limits the ability to move toward a rigorous, student-centered approach that both equips students with knowledge and skills and allows them to develop critical dispositions and creativity. As schools consider how to integrate teachers into their blended-learning designs, they have an exciting opportunity to think beyond a role that has time- and lecture-based elements geared for producing the factory workers of yesterday. Teachers can focus on implementing competency-based learning, such that students only move on when they have truly mastered a given concept, with the result that students who already understand something can make faster progress and escape boredom, and those who don't understand something won't fall further behind into bewilderment. Teachers also have an opportunity to spend more of their time focusing on helping students develop higher-order skills as online learning increasingly delivers content and instruction for students.

Fill the mentoring and coaching gap

A second observation concerns integrating teachers to help students fulfill their jobs. Because of some fundamental changes in society, students increasingly need teachers to serve as mentors and coaches, not only to help them build positive relationships and have fun with friends but also to help them succeed in life. With online learning delivering some part of a course's content and instruction, blended-learning programs create more time for teachers to fill this important role.

Schools cannot substitute for a stable, nurturing home. They can, however, help when children need a mentor or a coach. Many schools already do. In some cases, it's the only hope for a child to be successful. And even children from functional homes stand to benefit from outside mentors and coaches.

Schools across the country are integrating teachers as mentors and coaches in a variety of ways. For example, some schools assign students to have the same teacher for multiple years so that each student has a stable and continuous relationship in her life. Blended learning can help; because software can deliver lessons tailored to each student in a classroom of mixed ages and levels, it can free up schools to keep groups of students together with one teacher over many years, even as the students' academic abilities progress.

Outside of education, research shows that one of the most powerful things that the best managers do in high-performing organizations is to act as coaches. They coach their teams by giving feedback, meeting with team members for frequent one-on-ones, empowering their teams, and showing interest in and concern for each team member. That same opportunity is now available in schools. Blended learning makes it possible for teachers to shift away from directing and delivering instruction, and this in turn frees up their time to focus on doing the things that great coaches do.

Over time, we suspect that additional schools will turn to online learning to deliver content and instruction and then adjust their recruiting, training, and teacher evaluation processes to cultivate a team that includes many with a mentoring and coaching responsibility and fewer who lesson-plan for and lecture to an entire class in lockstep fashion.

> For more on how to harness the power of being a great mentor and coach, read "How to Create Higher Performing, Happier Classrooms in 7 Moves: A Playbook for Teachers" at *www.christenseninstitute.org/publications/playbook.* This playbook shares the findings of three researchers who set off to discover what K–12 schools can learn from the best-run organizations in America. Why are companies such as Zappos, Geico, and Google continually ranked among the best places to work if you want to be happy and successful? Could classroom teachers use similar strategies to improve their students' happiness and performance, not to mention their graduates' readiness to work in America's top organizations someday?
>
> The researchers—all of whom are former K–12 teachers—began by searching for strategies that successful managers in today's well-regarded organizations have in common. They found that the best managers in leading organizations do at least three things extraordinarily well: they empower their teams and do not micromanage, they are great coaches, and they emphasize accountability.

Check for understanding

Analyze the teacher roles

Watch the following video clips of blended learning in action—the first at an elementary school and the second at a high school. As you watch, take notes on the ways that the teacher roles are different from those of a traditional, factory-style classroom and the ways that teachers are spending their time.

Burnett Elementary School

www.wiley.com/go/blended16

USC Hybrid High School

www.wiley.com/go/blended19

Use the space here to record your observations about how teachers spend their time.

____

____

____

____

____

____

Check for understanding

Integrate teachers' roles to deliver the ideal student experience

Reflection questions

Recall the students' day-in-the-life and week-in-the-life narratives you crafted in Module 2.3. How do the teachers' roles fit into the narrative?

Do teachers move beyond planning and delivering whole-class lessons such that each individual student has more opportunities to feel successful each day, have fun with friends, and have more control over the time, place, path, and/or pace of their learning? If yes, how?

____

____

____

____

____

____

If not, why not? How might you adjust the student experience to help teachers move beyond planning and delivering whole-class lessons so that students don't progress in lockstep and have more opportunities to be successful?

____

____

____

____

____

____

Are teachers able to spend more time working on higher-order skills with students, as online learning delivers content and instruction? If yes, list some of the ways teachers are spending more time developing students' higher-order skills.

____

____

If teachers are not spending more time working on higher-order skills with students, why aren't they? How might you adjust the student experience to help teachers spend their time on these skills and applications of knowledge?

Do teachers have greater opportunities to mentor and coach students in your student experience so that students can have fun with their teachers? How? List some of the opportunities.

If not, why not? How might you adjust the student experience to help teachers have more time to mentor and coach students?

Identifying the key teacher roles

Given the student experience you want to create, what are the key roles teachers will need to play? Will they need to deliver face-to-face instruction? Provide face-to-face tutoring, guidance, and enrichment? Will they need to serve as an online teacher of record? Something else? List the roles here.

Draft your plan

Revising the student experience part of the plan

Having reflected on and responded to the previous questions, you may have already begun to adjust the student experience. If you would like to work on your revisions here, we have included space for you to rewrite a day in the life as well as a week in the life of a hypothetical student. As you revise, do your best to make sure your revised version matches up to an exceptional plan. To assist you, we've brought back the Student Experience Rubric from Module 2.3 but have also added two additional rows—"Competency-based learning" and "Mentorship and coaching"—so that you can take into account some of the teacher roles we've suggested in this module to help give students the experiences they need to be successful.

Student Experience Rubric

	Exceptional 3	Advanced 2	Basic 1	Inadequate 0
Design work	Designs a plan that **shows students' daily and weekly experiences** for each project from at least two perspectives; the plan includes **varied academic and social experiences**.	Provides a complete design, but it leaves **some question** about what the student experience will involve.	Provides a basic design, but it leaves **major questions** about what the student experience will involve.	Does not provide a tangible design beyond buzzwords.
Application of jobs-to-be-done theory	Designs a **comprehensive plan** that unlocks students' intrinsic motivations of feeling successful each day and having fun with friends while accounting for other barriers that require remediation (e.g., physical activity, work-related commitments).	Designs a plan that unlocks students' intrinsic motivations but **does not account for other barriers**.	Designs a plan, but it **does not unlock students' intrinsic motivations**.	Does not present any compelling set of experiences.

	Exceptional 3	Advanced 2	Basic 1	Inadequate 0
Link	Provides a **fully reasonable rationale** for why the new student experience will mitigate the problem identified in Section 1: Rallying Cry.	Presents a **mostly** reasonable link between the design and the problem.	Presents a **somewhat** reasonable link between the design and the problem.	Does not connect the design to the problem.
Competency-based learning	Incorporates the principles of competency-based learning to ensure that students will have the opportunity to work on higher-order skills and will not move in lockstep pace with the class at all times.	Incorporates the principles of competency-based learning, **but some parts are unrealistic or too vague**.	Attempts to incorporate competency-based learning, but **many parts are unrealistic or too vague**.	Does not incorporate the principles of competency-based learning, **OR** requires all students to move in lockstep.
Mentorship and coaching	Incorporates the principles of sound, one-on-one mentorship and coaching such that students will have the support and relationships they need to succeed in their particular circumstances.	Incorporates the principles of sound, one-on-one mentorship and coaching, but **some parts are unrealistic or too vague**.	Attempts to incorporate the principles of sound, one-on-one mentorship and coaching, but **many parts are unrealistic or too vague**.	Does not incorporate the principles of sound, one-on-one mentorship and coaching.

As in Module 2.3, for the other SMART goals you plan to tackle, use the blank sheets at the end of the workbook to draft these stories.

Day in the life of a hypothetical student

Week in the life of a hypothetical student

Content summary

Designing the teacher role from the teacher perspective

Now it's time to see how your current design stacks up from the teacher perspective. To gain teachers' buy-in, a redesigned school must benefit teachers as well. Teachers have personal jobs to do in their lives, and the magic happens when schools design experiences that fulfill the jobs of both students and teachers.

In the article "One More Time, How Do You Motivate Employees?" Frederick Herzberg's research reveals that employees can love and hate their jobs at the same time. This is possible because two sets of factors affect how people feel about their work. The first set, called *hygiene* factors, affects whether employees are dissatisfied with their jobs. Hygiene factors include things like salary, the work environment, supervision, and whether the organization's policies are tolerable. The second set, called *motivators*, determines the extent to which employees outright love their jobs. Motivators include feeling well recognized, having growth opportunities, and finding the work itself rewarding. *Blended* offers a deeper explanation of Herzberg's research. It's important to note that in Herzberg's categorization scheme, the opposite of job dissatisfaction is not job satisfaction, but just the absence of dissatisfaction. Similarly, the opposite of loving your job is not hating it, but the absence of loving it.

To help teachers perform better in their jobs, schools should work on improving the motivators; hygiene factors will only prevent teachers from leaving.

Check for understanding

Distinguishing a motivator from a hygiene factor

Next to each factor, circle whether it is a motivator or hygiene factor. The answers are in the appendix at the end of this module.

Achievement – Motivator or Hygiene factor

Supervision – Motivator or Hygiene factor

Company policy and administration – Motivator or Hygiene factor

Recognition – Motivator or Hygiene factor

Work itself – Motivator or Hygiene factor

Work conditions – Motivator or Hygiene factor

Personal life – Motivator or Hygiene factor

Responsibility – Motivator or Hygiene factor

Security – Motivator or Hygiene factor

Relationship with peers – Motivator or Hygiene factor

Reflection question

Of the motivators—achievement, recognition, the work itself, responsibility, advancement, and growth—which one do you most wish you had more of in your job today? Why?

Content summary

Integrating teacher motivators into blended designs

The traditional teaching job lacks many of the essential motivators. Teachers often work in isolation from other adults, which means there is little or no opportunity for recognition for their efforts. Just as in nursing, there is no real career track. Opportunities for increased responsibility and career advancement are slim. Aside from becoming the head of a department, the only other way for most teachers in most schools to move up in this line of work is, in fact, to stop teaching so that they can be "promoted" into an administrative job. And aside from occasional workshops or required training programs, teachers have limited opportunities for growth in the job after the first few years.

But blended learning creates an opportunity to blow apart that construct; if the blended program is designed well, the role of teachers can amplify motivators in ways that are difficult in the traditional, analog classroom. As you move forward with blended learning, here are five ways you can restructure the role of teachers to maximize their motivators:

1. Extending the reach of great teachers
2. Assigning individual teachers specialized responsibilities
3. Allowing teachers to teach in teams
4. Awarding teachers micro-credentials for the mastery of skills
5. Granting authority to blended-learning teams

Expand your strategy skills

Brainstorm implementation strategies

For each of the following strategies, brainstorm specific ways you might implement it in your design to amplify motivators for teachers.

1. Extending the reach of great teachers

   ____

   ____

   ____

2. Assigning individual teachers specialized responsibilities

   ____

   ____

   ____

3. Allowing teachers to teach in teams

   ____

   ____

   ____

4. Awarding teachers micro-credentials for the mastery of skills

   ____

   ____

   ____

5. Granting authority to blended-learning teams

   ____

   ____

   ____

View rubric and benchmarks

Incorporating the motivators in your design

Now it's time to think about the strategies that you plan to use to amplify the key motivators for teachers: achievement, recognition, the work itself, responsibility, advancement, and growth.

To assist you, the Amplifying Motivators Rubric distinguishes an inadequate incorporation of motivators (0) from a basic one (1), advanced (2), and exceptional (3).

Amplifying Motivators Rubric

	Exceptional 3	Advanced 2	Basic 1	Inadequate 0
Job motivators	Describes at least **two powerful motivators** that the design seeks to deliver to improve teachers' job satisfaction. Does not confuse a motivator with a hygiene factor.	Describes at least **one powerful motivator** that the design seeks to deliver to improve teachers' job satisfaction. Does not confuse a motivator with a hygiene factor.	Makes an effort to describe at least one motivator, but the design is **ordinary** from the teacher motivation perspective and does not allow for professional advancement.	Does not name any motivators.
Implementation strategy	Describes a concrete, realistic strategy for amplifying these motivators.	Describes a strategy for amplifying these motivators, but **small parts might be vague or unrealistic.**	Describes a strategy for amplifying these motivators, but **large parts are vague or unrealistic.**	**Does not describe a strategy** for amplifying the motivator(s) named.

Read through this example that a real school team developed to describe the strategies it plans to use, followed by our evaluation of those strategies according to the rubric.

Sample teacher experience statement

Teachers are our most valuable resource, and blended learning will help us support our teachers in ways we have never done before. Our plan allows us to amplify six motivators to bolster the teaching experience.

Responsibility

In our new model, teacher-leaders who master blended learning will develop district and regional responsibilities for training and supporting other teachers as well. They will also take the lead role in developing online content for all teachers and engage in implementation research and development.

Achievement, recognition, and advancement

To this end, as teachers flip their classrooms, they will gain new skill sets. Internally, those teachers who master the new craft will share their expertise with others, gain recognition from their peers and the administration as having specialized expertise, and we will give them new titles. Externally, we will have these teachers lead regional professional development sessions, present at national conferences, and earn micro-credentials.

> **Micro-credentials**
>
> Micro-credentials for teachers are growing in popularity. The theory is that just as students need personalized learning paths, teachers do as well for their professional development. Micro-credentials, in which teachers complete a specific activity to develop a critical competency for their role and earn a badge based on showing mastery of the skill, can help teachers document growing expertise and share their accomplishments in the classroom.
>
> To learn more and to see whether micro-credentials are available in your locality, check out the following:
>
> **BloomBoard**—*https://bloomboard.com/*
>
> **Digital Promise**—*http://digitalpromise.org/initiative/educator-micro-credentials/*
>
> **Getting Smart**—*http://www.gettingsmart.com/2016/03/building-micro-credential-momentum/*

Work itself

As teachers are freed up in-class to spend more time working individually with students and in small groups, they will have more opportunities to learn about each student's academic challenges and goals and about who they are as individuals outside the classroom. They will have more time to address each student's needs. And as students build motivation through success, engagement in the classroom will rise and behavior problems will decrease. All of this will bolster teacher satisfaction with and enjoyment in the work itself.

Growth

Our district has long offered a mix of internal experts and external resources to help teachers develop their craft. We can take the same approach for blended-learning professional development by having teachers learn from the blended-learning coordinator, other teachers, and high-quality external resources such as online professional development models or other outside experts. We know that our blended-learning teachers, like the students they love, all learn at different speeds, have different strengths and weaknesses, and will have varying levels of comfort with implementation. Therefore, we will use similar strategies to differentiate PD so that all our teachers can find success. Additionally, all teachers will be part of a community of practice that allows them to form strong relationships, learn from one another, and set a precedent for collaborating around innovation within our district.

Professional development for blended learning

There are an increasing number of resources available to support teachers with professional development that is personalized for their distinct needs and for preparing them to teach in a blended-learning environment. Check out the following:

BetterLesson—*http://betterlesson.com/blended-learning*

Coursera—*https://www.coursera.org/learn/blended-learning*

The Friday Institute—*http://www.fi.ncsu.edu/focus-areas/education-workforce-development/leadership-in-blended-learning/*

The Highlander Institute (Sample playlist for educators)—*https://www.tes.com/lessons/_IXCDHStjLX9Kw/chariho-district-blended-learning*

The Learning Accelerator—*http://learningaccelerator.org/recommendations-and-resources-for-school-districts/human-capital/professional-development*

Ready to Blend—The Blended Learning Live! Experience—*https://www.readytoblend.com/*

Relay University—*http://www.relay.edu/blend-today*

Scoring explanation

This is a strong answer. It names at least two powerful motivators—in this case, six—that the design seeks to deliver to improve teachers' job satisfaction. It does not confuse a motivator with a hygiene factor. It also identifies a compelling strategy that the team will implement to amplify these motivators alongside a realistic plan for implementing them. We give this 6 points.

Practice evaluating

Teacher experience statements

Rate the following statements on a 0–3 scale (0 = inadequate, 1 = basic, 2 = advanced, 3 = exceptional) using the Amplifying Motivators Rubric. Explain your reasons why. Our answers are in the appendix at the end of this module.

Statement 1

Our plan incorporates all of the primary motivators for teachers to love their jobs.

Achievement

We think bringing blended learning into our district will allow teachers to be reborn into the rock stars they were in their first years of teaching—filled with enthusiasm and idealism. Because blended learning will be a new concept to our entire staff, everyone will start together. We are hopeful that teachers will help us draft a personalized learning plan for their own self-improvement as educators, in the spirit of exciting new beginnings. By establishing a vision of short-term attainable goals, we are confident that we can steadily increase active participation in professional development sessions and self-study among our teachers. We will give teachers the recognition they earn for figuring out what works best for them and for having the willingness to advance their thinking for the benefit of their students (and other teachers). Our support for and recognition of our teachers will help ease the growing pains that can come with change. Those who are the early adopters of the blended-learning initiative will more visibly fail and succeed, but failing with support through collaboration will become a safe learning moment—proof that failing is the first step toward figuring it out.

Recognition

We will recognize teachers through a teacher of the month and year at each campus, and those teachers will be featured in our town newspaper and on our district website. We will also post celebratory "attempts" blogs on our district website, with links posted on our district Twitter and Facebook accounts. These "attempts" will include successes and failures (with teacher approval) as an important way to share our transition stories around the district and with other sites exploring blended models. We will create a classroom badges program to post outside each teacher's classroom door as a way to proudly display each teacher's achievements, products mastered, and student brags. By making the badges visible to everyone on campus, both teachers and students can easily identify whom to seek for help.

Responsibility and Advancement

In time, we plan to work out a structure that will allow teachers to choose where their strengths are best utilized and provide a spark or a carrot for those needing one to chase. At this point, a scenario is envisioned where we have three different distinctions or "tiers" of teachers. Learning Guide (Level I), Learning Planner (Level II), and Learning Expert (Level III) positions will each come with different distinctions, pay grades, and responsibilities in order to give teachers the opportunity to strive for something greater. In most current scenarios, we move our strongest teachers out of the classroom and into administrative roles because we think it will give them magic powers to pass on to the rest of the staff. As we know, that plan does not always work out that way, but we would like to create a system where teachers could progress as professionals without having to go into administration as the next logical step.

Growth

Professional development in our district will also change based on what we learn about blended learning. It is difficult to find time for PD during the school year. During the school year, most PD will take the shape of an Enriched Virtual model. Summers will allow for more face-to-face training, but these virtual courses will remain active as well. We will work to create online sessions that are self-paced and on-demand. Just after teachers complete their PD online session, they will meet with administrators in a quick follow-up, face-to-face meeting to check for understanding and elaborate where necessary. Surveys will be an integral part of the post-PD plan to re-shape any areas where understanding was weak or unclear.

Work Itself

We recently surveyed our teachers about blended learning, analyzed the honest opinions and ideas we received, and identified common strands across the district. Our teachers are:

1. Frustrated with the amount of time they have to work with students outside of whole-group instruction, so our blended design will give them more opportunities for small-group and one-on-one interaction with students.
2. Frustrated with how difficult it is to differentiate instruction for students, when the range of student needs spreads from really low to really high, so our blended design will give them a greater ability to reach each student where he or she is in his or her learning.
3. Ready for something different and positive through blended learning, so our blended design will accordingly refresh their outlook on teaching by tackling the first two aspects of their frustration with the work itself.

We will begin to build our support structure by training our campus leadership teams first. They will be critical in helping develop an evaluation system that fosters our teachers' continuous growth.

Your score: ______________________________

Why?

____

____

Statement 2

We have intentionally designed our blended-learning initiative to maximize positive motivators for participating teachers. The following *new* strategies will be used to promote additional motivators.

Autonomy and space to innovate

To promote autonomy and encourage innovation, the district will remove some of the traditional barriers to innovation, such as bell and class schedules and administration of some of the required district-level student assessments. Allowing for differentiation in classroom structure, instructional delivery modalities, and means of assessment will provide a true departure from traditional teaching. Participating teachers will have great flexibility outside of the district's structured scope and sequence plans and will not be mandated to attend district and campus level staff development days; instead, they will have the flexibility to work with other blended-learning teachers and to receive targeted professional development that applies to their new classroom approaches. Participating teachers will also receive support from a personalized learning mentor, share conference times with other blended-learning teachers, and work closely with those teachers to plan and review data as a team.

Innovation Task Force participation

This united group of teachers will have dedicated time to work and plan together throughout the year. They will develop a means of communicating challenges and solutions from their implementation experiences to share with others. This task force will become the "trainers of trainers," providing the needed support to expand and scale the program to other grade levels at their own schools and other schools across the district. Their classrooms will become observation rooms for others to visit. We will develop a YouTube channel to post videos of best practice strategies and lessons from their classrooms to allow them to be recognized for their pioneering spirit and to share successes and lessons learned with others.

Potential

We move teachers into Personal Learning Coach positions as they are added. We recognize their potential to become great coaches as the program expands.

Your score: ______________________

Why?

____

____

____

____

____

____

Statement 3

The most important motivating factor for our district's teachers is the work itself. Based on an extensive survey across our district, we learned that 92% of our teachers love working directly with our district's students, but feel frustrated at how many students are either lagging in their understanding of the material or bored with the level of it. Personalized instruction and attention are critical needs for all students, and we think blended learning can give our teachers the boost they need in their work itself. By moving away from teacher-centered and generalized instruction to the student-centered and personalized learning made possible through technology, our classrooms will become places of individual and small-group work, where the teacher can move easily among students and address their different concerns. Because the learning programs will be able to track and chart students' progress in real time, teachers will be empowered to respond to each student's needs immediately and accurately, thus increasing their own satisfaction in their role.

Your score: ____________________

Why?

____

____

____

____

____

____

Draft your plan

Design the teacher experience

Now it's your turn. Draft the teacher experience section of your blended-learning plan. Remember, an exceptional description will name the specific motivators that your design seeks to amplify for teachers and will identify at least two new and compelling strategies that the team will implement to amplify these motivators.

Use the blank sheets at the end of the workbook to draft the teacher experience section for your other SMART goals.

Before moving on, remember to self-assess your work. Look at the Amplifying Motivators Rubric and see how you'd score yourself. Keep working until you would give yourself a 6!

APPENDIX

Check for understanding: Distinguishing a motivator from a hygiene factor

Achievement – Motivator

Supervision – Hygiene factor

Company policy and administration – Hygiene factor

Recognition – Motivator

Work itself – Motivator

Work conditions – Hygiene factor

Personal life – Hygiene factor

Responsibility – Motivator

Security – Hygiene factor

Relationship with peers – Hygiene factor

Our evaluation of teacher experience statements

Statement 1

Our score: 6

This is an outstanding answer that names at least two powerful motivators (in this case, it names them all!) that the design seeks to deliver to improve teachers' job satisfaction. It does not confuse a motivator with a hygiene factor. It also identifies a compelling strategy that the team will implement to amplify these motivators and presents a realistic plan for amplifying them.

Statement 2

Our score: 4

This advanced statement makes an effort to name at least one motivator, but the design is somewhat flat and ordinary from the teacher motivation perspective.

The strategy is mostly compelling and realistic for amplifying the motivators(s).

Statement 3

Our score: 2

This is a basic answer that makes an effort to name at least one motivator—the work itself—but the design is only mostly flat and ordinary from the teacher motivation perspective. The strategy of enabling one-on-one and small-group work through the use of personalized-learning technology is somewhat compelling and realistic for amplifying the work-itself motivator.

Physical and Virtual Environment

Key objectives

- Complete a technology audit and identify some key takeaways
- Analyze an existing software strategy through the lenses of interdependence and modularity theory and operational fit; identify ways to improve the strategy
- Anticipate the changes that blended learning requires of physical space, and plan accordingly

Content summary

Avoiding a "tech mess"

With your design for the student and teacher experiences starting to take shape, it's time to turn your attention to the physical and virtual environments that you need to set up to provide the stage and backdrop. This task is both easier and more complicated than it was a decade ago. It's easier because the disruptive innovation—online learning—has gradually improved over time. Devices, learning software, and learning management systems have gotten better. More places have Internet access. More schools are wired for technology. At the same time, managing these high-tech environments has become more complicated. Many schools find themselves with a variety of laptops, desktops, and tablets; an assortment of software licenses and apps that do not fit together with any apparent rhyme or reason; and physical facilities that seem increasingly antiquated for today's world.

This module of the workbook helps you analyze the infrastructure that you already have in place and rationalize your plan for strategic investments in technology and facilities going forward. After working through it, you will be better positioned either to avoid a so-called tech mess at your site or to untangle one if it already exists.

Take inventory

Physical and virtual environment audit

To begin, it's helpful to take inventory of what you currently have. That will allow you to analyze what's working and what needs to change to create the best environment possible for your blended program. Before you go any further, we recommend that you take the time to complete the following basic audit. If you are doing more than one project, go through this module from start to finish for each project, one at a time.

Even if you are not a technology whiz, you should be able to complete this audit, as the questions are mostly nontechnical. That said, if you have the option of getting support from IT personnel in your organization, take advantage of it. The audit is a good section to delegate, and it requires a significant time commitment.

You can complete your audit here in the workbook—or we've also provided a way for you to complete the audit using Google Sheets.

To use Google Sheets, go to bit.ly/BlendedEnvironAudit and click on the "Make a copy" icon. A new page will open with your own copy of the table for the physical and virtual environment audit that we use in this workbook.

Physical and virtual environment audit

Date:			
	Year 1	**Year 2**	**Year 3**
Name(s) of school(s) implementing project 1			
Number of classrooms participating			
Number of students participating			
Number of teachers participating			
Software audit ***Complete this form for each online course, product, or set of modules that you use. Also complete it for your learning management system (LMS). Some questions will not apply to the LMS.***			
Vendor name (Enter the teacher's or team's name if this content was built in-house)			

Date:	
Name of course or product	
1. **Grade level**—What grade levels or ages is the content designed to serve?	
2. **Content**—What subjects are taught, and what is the instructional purpose (e.g., fluency, comprehension, concept introduction)?	
3. **Full-time or supplemental**—How many hours of content are in this course? If it's only enough to supplement other content, how many hours does this software provide?	
4. **Price**—What are the costs? Include all development costs, licensing fees, setup fees, etc. Note if fees are one-time or periodic. Is any unused professional development remaining on the contract?	
5. **Student experience**—Can students see where they are, what they have accomplished, and what they need to do next? Can they see their metrics and get real-time feedback? Can they choose among different pathways? Is it engaging and intrinsically motivating the entire time? Can they pause the lesson and then later pick up where they left off? What is their overall level of control?	
6. **Adaptability and assignability**—Does the software slow down and speed up automatically in response to student performance? What happens when a student gets a question wrong—does the software provide easier content and hints? Can teachers select which modules to assign?	
7. **Data**—Does the software provide actionable data for teachers? Does it help connect the online and offline learning? Who owns the data—you or the provider? Does the provider provide access to the data you need in a user-friendly format?	
8. **Efficacy**—What evidence is there that the software has helped other students achieve the learning outcomes you desire? How long does it take?	

Date:	
9. **Target population**—Which students benefit from the program (e.g., special education, English language learners, etc.)? For whom would the content NOT be accessible?	
10. **Flexibility**—Is the software cloud-based to allow students to work from anywhere?	
11. **Compatibility**—Is the software compatible with your devices? Is it behaving in the way you need with your other devices and software systems? Will it work with future devices you might want to use?	
12. **Alignment**—Is the software aligned to your learning standards? What percentage of grade-level standards are covered?	
13. **Provisioning**—How easy is it for you to provision new users with usernames and passwords by connecting directly from your student information system to the software?	
14. **Single sign-on**—Does the software integrate easily into a single sign-on process so that students only have to enter their username and password one time?	
15. **Expiration**—State when your license expires, if applicable.	
16. **Feedback**—Provide evaluation data from focus groups of students and teachers.	
LMS-specific questions:	
17. **Social experience**—Does the LMS provide a social experience for teachers and students? Evaluate.	
18. **Content creation**—Describe the LMS's ability to create content and tests.	
19. **Gradebook**—Describe the LMS's gradebook functionality.	
20. **Sharing resources**—Describe any functionality the LMS offers related to sharing, tagging, and rating resources.	

Date:	
Middleware audit ***List any tools that you use as a bridge to connect applications, such as data integration services and student information systems.***	
Platform or tool	**Purpose and comments**
Device audit ***Complete this form for any device that you use. Additional information that may prove helpful to document includes model numbers, serial numbers, and warranty information. Include that information if you have time and need.***	
Manufacturer name	
Product name	
Form factor (laptop, desktop, tablet, mobile device)	
Operating system	
Number of devices	
Useful life (estimate of the period of time remaining during which this device will provide benefit)	
Evaluation feedback from focus groups of students and teachers	

Date:		
Other hardware ***(Printers, external monitors, external keyboards, laptop carts, laptop bags, iPad covers, etc.)***		
Product	**Quantity**	**Description**

Physical facilities	
Availability and speed of Wi-Fi in school(s) of implementation. State upload and download speed as megabits per second (Mbps) per user. If you don't know this information, go to http://www.schoolspeedtest.org/ to find out.	
Description of any dead zones without Wi-Fi access in the building(s).	
Availability of electrical sockets that can handle devices in schools of implementation, taking into account whether the sockets are blocked off by furniture.	
Description of computer or media lab(s), if any, in school(s) of implementation.	
Description of any spaces that could be converted into large, open learning spaces in school(s) of implementation.	
Summary of furniture in school(s) of implementation. Provide a general impression of the number of single desks versus group tables and whether the furniture is moveable or stationary.	

Draw your conclusions

What are your initial takeaways?

Before you go deeper into analyzing your audit results, take a moment to summarize your preliminary observations. What assets do you already have available to you that you want to be sure to leverage? Where are there obvious misfits and gaps?

Several of the questions on this worksheet ask you to rate the infrastructure that's already in place. Use this audit rating scale.

Audit Rating Scale

	Exceptional 3	Advanced 2	Basic 1	Inadequate 0
Existing infrastructure	Enough to meet our needs completely and a great fit with our design	Enough to get us **most** of the way there and **tolerably matched** to our design	Enough to get us started, but **will need investment** to support our design	Nonexistent, unusable, and/or a total misfit with our design; a "**tech mess**"

Software and LMS observations

1. Using the 0–3 Audit Rating Scale, how do you rate the software and LMS already available to you for your blended program? ______

2. What are the main strengths of your existing software and LMS? What are the top opportunities to take advantage of with the software and LMS you already have?

______

______

______

______

______

3. What are the gaps with your software and LMS, given the number of students and teachers who will be part of your blended program by Year 3 and your intended design?

______

______

Middleware observations

1. Using the 0–3 Audit Rating Scale, how do you rate the middleware already available to you for your blended program? ____________________

2. What are the main opportunities to leverage with your existing middleware?

3. What are the gaps with your middleware?

Hardware observations

1. Using the 0–3 Audit Rating Scale, how do you rate the devices already available to you for your blended program? ____________________

2. What are the main opportunities to leverage with your existing devices?

3. What are the gaps with your devices?

Other hardware observations

1. Using the 0–3 Audit Rating Scale, how do you rate the other hardware already available to you for your blended program? ______

2. What are the main opportunities to leverage with your other hardware?

3. What are the gaps with your other hardware?

Physical facilities observations

1. Using the 0–3 Audit Rating Scale, how do you rate the physical facilities already available to you for your blended program? ______

2. What are the main opportunities to leverage with your facilities?

3. What are the gaps with your facilities?

Content summary

Interdependent and modular product architecture

Now let's take your analysis a level deeper by considering the probable future of online content and applying that lens to your strategy. We'll begin by reviewing a few big ideas about interdependent and modular system architecture.

Some products have an *interdependent* architecture. The design and fabrication of part A affects the way that parts B and C must be built, and vice versa. How these parts interact with each other is also not always certain. The company making the product must integrate its operations to control every aspect of the design and production of each of these parts or else risk encountering manufacturing surprises and performance issues. Integrating to control every element optimizes functionality and reliability. The drawback, however, is that customization in an interdependent architecture is prohibitively expensive. It costs a lot to swap out one part for another.

Other products have a *modular* architecture. The components in a modular architecture fit together in such well-understood and well-defined ways that it does not matter who makes each component, as long as it meets predetermined standards or specifications. Modular components are plug compatible; it's easy to swap in and out different components to configure a customized result. Modularity therefore offers a lot of flexibility and customization. The drawback, however, is that modularity does not offer as high a level of performance and reliability compared to interdependent architecture.

The implications for software

If you're tasked with selecting a software strategy, you are faced with four options in terms of interdependence and modularity.

Strategy 1: Do it yourself (DIY)

One of the first questions most blended leaders ask is whether to "build or buy." Should schools build their own online courses and content—a choice that is more integrated—or use off-the-shelf content that a third party has developed—the more modular option? The main advantages of the DIY strategy are the opportunities to control quality, design the content according to local standards and testing requirements, avoid the high cost of premium third-party alternatives, and allow face-to-face teachers to be the source of content and instruction. In addition, some educators enjoy developing the skill set of building an online course. The main reason some schools decide against the DIY strategy is that they have neither the time, money, nor in-house expertise required to develop proprietary content that is high quality. They see the growing libraries of third-party courses and decide to leave the software development to software developers, rather than try to build that competency themselves.

Strategy 2: Use one outside provider

Many schools decide to use one outside provider per course or subject. There are a wide range of these providers—from K12, Inc. and Apex Learning to Dreambox Learning and Istation. Although using a single provider doesn't give schools the customization they may prefer within a course, the simplicity and reliability of this strategy are worth the trade-off. These schools never worry about having to coordinate data across multiple providers. Furthermore, some of the software is becoming remarkably adaptive, engaging, and aligned to the latest research in cognitive science. Integrated software has its drawbacks, however. One is that the technology tends to be expensive if it's any good, particularly if it is going to offer customization. Also, students who would benefit from a different approach have no option but to use the single solution.

Strategy 3: Combine multiple providers

Some schools decide that they do not want to develop their own content, but that they need a more flexible solution than relying on a single provider for an entire course or subject. They want modularity within the course to allow for a variety of pathways for each student. In response, they patch together several proprietary programs into a unified platform, ideally with a single dashboard that provides summary data for the student and teacher. The attraction of this strategy is that a more modular world for online content gives schools greater flexibility to personalize learning. But the flipside is that teachers often find that these cobbled-together solutions are a headache to operate. Teachers struggle to get data out of the systems, and the standards and data from one provider do not align easily to the standards and the data from another.

Strategy 4: Use a facilitated network

A new wave of disruptive innovation is emerging and carries the potential to swing the industry toward full modularity. Software platforms are emerging that facilitate the development, sharing, and curating of user-generated content in modular bites. A prime example of this is the Khan Academy platform, which hosts over 100,000 exercise problems and a growing library of thousands of video tutorials. The platform is open and nonproprietary; other software can easily interface and be compatible with it. Other so-called facilitated networks like this are emerging that allow parents, teachers, and students to offer microinstruction to other parents, teachers, and students.

The arrival of facilitated networks brings two main benefits. The first is hypercustomization. Modular platforms will one day amass hundreds of millions of microtutorials, on-demand assessments, and other learning objects that users will be able to browse and select to assemble together customized courses based on the needs of each learner. The second benefit is affordability.

In contrast to proprietary, integrated software, the content that's available through facilitated networks is, on average, much less expensive to make and oftentimes free to use.

The disadvantage in planning to use a facilitated network strategy is that, to date, there is no clear winner among the emerging facilitated network platforms—and all have significant disadvantages. A few systems, such as Khan Academy's platform, Agilix's Buzz, Summit's Personalized Learning Platform, Gooru, Core Learning Exchange, and Schoology, facilitate aspects of content creation and delivery; however, the market still awaits a platform that makes it simple for educators and students to create or upload, share, review, tag, and sell user-generated and third-party content.

Resources to help choose software

Common Sense Media—A collection of independent reviews, age ratings, and other information for all types of media, including movies, books, TV, games, apps, and websites.

www.commonsensemedia.org

EdCredible—Real end-user K–12 product reviews to save districts money, time, and resources.

https://www.edcredible.com/

EdSurge Product Index—A database of over two thousand edtech products, which can be filtered by category, age of learner, curriculum type, tech requirements, cost, and usage.

www.edsurge.com/product-reviews

Learning List—Alignment reports and independent reviews of textbooks and online resources, searchable by usage, formats, and alignment to standards.

www.learninglist.com

Noodle Markets—A database of education products, services, and vendors, along with tools to streamline the procurement process.

https://www.noodlemarkets.com/

Expand your strategy skills

Imagine that . . .

Suppose that you had the funds to pursue any of the four strategies: DIY, use one outside provider, combine multiple providers, or use a facilitated network. Which of the four strategies would fit your design the best? Why?

Would there be any drawbacks to implementing that strategy? Explain.

Content summary

Changes to physical facilities

In an aesthetic sense, one could argue that the traditional architecture of factory-type schools has coalesced around an integrated design that—although reliable and orderly—has little to offer in terms of openness, flexibility, or modularity. For many, particularly those who are seeking to bring sustaining improvements to the traditional classroom model through Station Rotations, Lab Rotations, and Flipped Classrooms, the basic layout of standard classrooms may be perfectly adequate. Many blended programs, however, are choosing to rearrange their furniture and physical space to align with the principles of student agency, flexibility, and choice that are at the core of their new models.

The following examples illustrate how schools are changing their physical facilities to support their efforts to personalize learning.

- Khan Lab School, an independent school founded by the renowned Sal Khan, has roughly one hundred students, ages five to fourteen. It has converted the bottom floor of an office park into a learning studio. There are no interior walls in the studio; it feels more like a one-room schoolhouse, in keeping with Khan's book *The One-World Schoolhouse,* than like a standard school building. The open space gives students the flexibility they need to complete collaborative term projects, such as starting a greeting card business or building a computer from scratch.
- Kelly Kosuga, a ninth-grade Algebra I teacher at Cindy Avitia High School, an Alpha Public School, has found that her two whiteboards were helpful to her Flex model. When students are not making progress on their online IXL program, she calls them to the whiteboards and asks them to show their work. That allows her to see their work written big, which helps her spot their errors. It also helps students feel her attention and

stay focused. Ms. Kosuga now has whiteboards for all of the walls of her room because they are so helpful in supporting her work as a coach in her Flex environment.

- The New Learning Academy in Kep County, England, features at the heart of its design a learning plaza large enough to house 120 students. The school uses the flexibility of the plaza for five activity modes: (1) Campfire—allows for class work; (2) Watering Hole—allows for small-group work; (3) Cave—allows for self-study; (4) Studio—allows for projects; and (5) Multiple intelligences—allows for a mix of modes.

Expand your strategy skills

Imagine that . . .

Watch this clip. The Avenues: World School provides students with an open learning environment to support its Station Rotation.

www.wiley.com/go/blended6

Suppose that you had the funds to pursue any design for your physical facilities to align them perfectly to the experience you are trying to create. In the space provided, sketch out your before and after pictures. An example is provided.

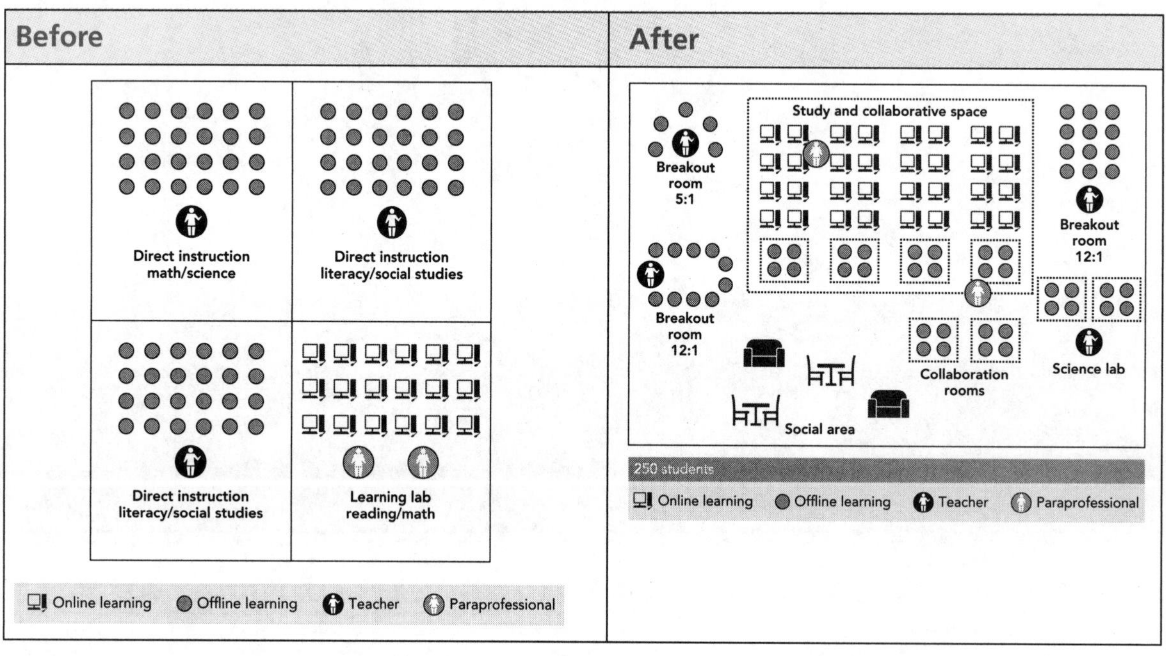

Before	After

Suppose that your funds are more limited (which is probably the case!). Imagine the smaller changes you might want to make to your facilities and furniture to accommodate your design. Sketch and label them here.

View rubric and benchmarks

Planning for the physical and virtual environment

You've completed your audit and imagined some of the elements of your ideal design, using the theory of interdependence and modularity to clarify your options. Now let's formalize your thoughts into a succinct plan.

The Physical and Virtual Environment Rubric highlights the aspects of an exceptional physical and virtual environment plan and distinguishes an exceptional plan (3) from one that is advanced (2), basic (1), or inadequate (0).

Physical and Virtual Environment Rubric

	Exceptional 3	Advanced 2	Basic 1	Inadequate 0
Audit	Provides a **full summary** of a formal audit report that examines the quantity and useful life of hardware and software assets, the quality of Wi-Fi, and the availability of suitable facilities for the blended program(s).	Provides a summary of a formal audit report, but it is **missing some key summative information**.	Provides some data about the existing environment, but it has **big data gaps**.	Audit report is **missing** or mostly incomplete.
Analysis of audit	Evidences an **accurate and thorough** understanding of the ways that the existing environment already accommodates the proposed blended-learning design and the ways in which it will need to change.	Evidences an adequate understanding of these issues, but one part of the analysis is **not thorough** and/or has **inaccuracies**.	Evidences some thought about these issues, but the analysis is largely **superficial** and/or **inaccurate**.	Analysis is **missing OR** does not relate to the audit.

	Exceptional 3	Advanced 2	Basic 1	Inadequate 0
Vision for improvement	Presents a new vision for the physical and virtual environment that **aligns neatly** with and **supports** the new learning design.	Presents a new vision for the environment that is aligned to the learning design, but **one part of the learning design might not be supported.**	Presents a vision for the environment that is **largely incomplete**.	Vision for improvement is **missing** or does not support the new learning design.

Read through this example of a physical and virtual environment plan, followed by our evaluation of the plan according to the rubric.

Sample physical and virtual environment plan

Our full audit report is available upon request. This is the summary of key findings. We found that the physical and virtual environments of our schools are already 60 percent sufficient to provide Lab Rotation and Individual Rotation models of blended learning for high school math and English/language arts. Classes have adequate space and furniture, and half of the schools have sufficient Chromebooks and carts. Many classrooms are already experimenting with online adaptive content, though not in a formalized manner. The 40 percent preparedness gap comes from (1) lack of reliable Internet, (2) inadequate number of Chromebooks in three of the schools, and (3) lack of interschool alignment on software choice and use of data.

Virtual infrastructure

Schools' network capacities and existing technology:

A. Finding (Software). Schools use a mix of software providers for math and reading (see full audit). All schools are experimenting with online adaptive content at varying levels of use. Students show high levels of investment in online content, especially software with avatars and other game-like features. Students and teachers benefit from the clear pathways that are assignable. Teachers have begun to use data to inform instruction.

B. Recommendation. Schools should align around using program X [name withheld] for Algebra I and Geometry and program Y for upper level courses. We will need to identify suitable programs for English and AP courses. Focusing on 1–2 core programs will allow us to share best practices and compare results between schools. Schools must explicitly train teachers in the use of data provided by these sites.

C. Finding (Devices and Hardware). Four of seven schools are close to having adequate devices and hardware to support blended learning. Their Chromebooks were purchased recently and are in excellent condition. Three of the seven schools do not have the devices and hardware needed to support blended learning at the scale of the models we propose. Chromebooks and carts at all schools were in good condition, and schools have built expectations and culture around digital citizenship responsibility.

D. Recommendation. Chromebooks are the optimal choice for our blended-learning models because of their low cost, 8-hour battery life, and quick start-up time. The three schools without Chromebooks in English classrooms will need to order enough Chromebooks and carts for each student to use one during class. Teachers should continue their lessons on digital citizenship and responsibility.

E. Finding (Maintenance). Our district has an IT department of 10 professionals serving 15 schools. Schools do not have internal IT departments to handle breaks/fixes and must submit tickets to central office to repair computers and carts. Many staff at schools know how to handle basic technology malfunctions. Older students are computer literate as well.

F. Recommendation. Ideally, each set of schools would have an in-house IT specialist to handle broken devices. However, schools can make strategic use of staff with IT skills by designating a break/fix person(s). Schools will also look into hiring work-study students from nearby colleges and universities for minimal impact on budget. With the current maintenance landscape, it becomes even more important for teachers to ensure students have clear expectations for Chromebook use.

Physical infrastructure

A. Finding (Wi-Fi Access). At schools surveyed, the majority of classrooms shared a wireless access point (WAP) with at least one other classroom. One school has a WAP in each classroom. Many schools experience network crashes due to overuse. All but one school have a 48-port switch to connect computers and improve network efficiency.

B. Recommendation. We must install a 48-port switch in the one school without one to ensure Internet reliability. Ideally, schools will have a WAP in each classroom. Our first priority is to install a WAP in each classroom used by the math cohorts so that classrooms do not experience breaks in connectivity.

C. Finding. The schools surveyed had sufficient space to accommodate classes up to 32 students. Classes that would use an Individual Rotation model were equipped with folding tables that are easily configurable. Classrooms have limited electrical outlets. Some classrooms that will be used have desks attached to chairs that are hard to reconfigure. Facilities are a mix of building and modulars. Teachers have desks with chairs.

D. Recommendation. Exchange desks attached to chairs for flat tables or flat, light desks that can be easily reconfigured to allow for group and/or individual workspaces. Space is adequate, but not ample, so teachers must be efficient with use of space and work actively to reduce clutter. Classrooms with few outlets must make use of their charging carts, as computers will not be able to be plugged in individually. Modular classrooms will be able to make excellent use of wall space for blended-learning trackers, as walls are made of a bulletin board–like material. Add or designate a table for small-group instruction; consider removing the teacher desk to conserve space and replacing it with a small group table.

Scoring explanation

This is a very strong statement that we give 8 points according to the rubric. It provides a high-level summary of the formal audit report along all dimensions of hardware, software, Wi-Fi, and facilities. It shows an accurate understanding of the ways that the existing environment already accommodates the proposed blended-learning design and the ways in which it will need to change. It is thorough, but the statement would be strengthened with more information about how the recommendations support and align to the Lab Rotation and Individual Rotation design that the team envisions. We deduct 1 point based on that item. Note that the rubric does not penalize teams that have a long way to go in terms of building their physical and virtual environments. That's not what matters. The key is being able to analyze the existing infrastructure, whatever it may be, and make a sound plan for improvement.

Practice evaluating

Physical and virtual environment plans

Rate the following physical and virtual environment plans on a 0–3 scale of using the Physical and Virtual Environment Rubric. Explain your reasons why. Our answers are in the appendix at the end of this module.

Statement 1

Technology (devices and Wi-Fi access)

Because of visionary district leaders and community and Board of Trustees support, we are a technology-rich district. Every classroom has a projector, interactive whiteboard, and document camera. Five schools are part of the district's 1:1 technology device initiative, meaning that every student is issued either a Dell Venue Windows 8 tablet with a keyboard and stylus or a Dell Latitude laptop. Each of these devices has a 3–5 year useful life expectancy, and the district has planned for replacement of these devices, as needed, but no later than the 2019–2020 school year. Supported by a Cisco wireless network, 100% of the classrooms at each of the five selected campuses have the capacity to support 25–30 simultaneous Wi-Fi connections, and the district has a 3G Internet connection.

Software licenses

Pilot program students and staff have access to Google Classroom Tools and Gmail. We also have an assortment of content-driven software and online subscriptions, including: [vendor names withheld]. In addition, the majority of students' textbooks are available online. As part of the pilot initiative, the district will utilize the Northwest Education Association's (NWEA's) Measures of Academic Progress (MAP), which is designed to measure students' academic strengths and weaknesses via an adaptive, online assessment. Staff, students, and parents will also have access to an online platform that will be the primary source of content delivery and assessment for the initiative.

Facilities

The first three sites are state-of-the-art, new schools that were planned and constructed with personalized learning in mind. Classrooms are designed as flexible learning spaces equipped with collaborative learning furniture. These schools also have both large- and small-group, flexible learning spaces throughout the building. The remaining two campuses that will be part of the pilot initiative will require new furniture to provide the necessary collaborative and flexible learning spaces, but are well-equipped with the technology and infrastructure that are needed to facilitate the district's pilot initiative.

Analysis of strengths and gaps

As outlined above, the district, including the five selected pilot schools, has a solid wireless network infrastructure, a multitude of online curriculum resources, a competent IT support staff, and abundant student devices and accessories to support personalized learning. We have been thoughtful in planning for all aspects of personalized/blended learning, including providing additional power charging stations to ensure that students can work throughout the day on their devices. One gap for the district is the lack of home Internet access for close to 25 percent of our students. Knowing that home access is crucial to ensure that students can continue to work and learn whenever it is convenient for them, district officials recently submitted to the Board of Trustees a plan for approval of funding to install district-owned Wi-Fi towers around our city. The plan was approved, paving the way for our district to be one of the few districts in the nation that provides free Wi-Fi to its students and their families via district-owned towers. Tower installation will begin in January and is expected to be completed by May.

The physical space in some of the pilot initiative's selected schools will require minor redesign to provide more open, flexible, and collaborative learning spaces. Some furniture will be needed to create the kinds of spaces that will facilitate and complement the personalized/blended-learning environment at two of our sites. There may also be the need at one or more of the schools to move some classroom locations to ensure that teachers participating in the pilot initiative can be near each other to help facilitate peer tutoring opportunities between classrooms, provide space for students to work collaboratively, and allow for better teacher-to-teacher communication and community building.

Priorities and improvement plans

The priority is to purchase collaborative furniture for the selected grade-level teams. Principals will then make accommodations to move the grade-level teams' classrooms near each other to promote a supportive community of learning. A detailed plan and schedule for classroom design and set-up will be developed and put into action, following approval of funding. As mentioned previously, another priority of the district is to provide home Internet access to students. The district began building Wi-Fi towers throughout the city in January. This project shows the district's commitment to providing students with personalized/blended-learning opportunities that can be extended beyond the walls of classrooms and into students' homes through 24/7 access to online instructional opportunities. The district is working diligently to eliminate all barriers that prevent students from learning to their fullest potential by providing devices, software, and Internet access. As new needs arise, the district is committed to finding and implementing viable solutions to ensure the optimal physical and virtual infrastructure and space for the effective planning, implementation, and eventual scaling up of personalized/ blended learning across the district.

Your score: ______________________

Why?

____

____

____

____

____

____

Statement 2

Audit: The pilot elementary school for our Station Rotation blended-learning initiative has an old building with a physical structure of traditional classrooms and hallways. Each classroom is organized according to teachers' preferences for their students. Two classrooms have rows of desks, with a rug and beanbag reading corner; most classrooms have desks arranged in groupings of four or six to allow collaborative work among students; these classrooms also include reading corners. Currently, our school uses Apple products, with a ratio of 1:6 for iPads to students. The iPads live at school, given the challenges to securing them outside of the school building. All teachers have a laptop, which they sometimes share with students for access to online content.

Analysis: Historically, we have had difficulty getting the most value out of the iPads, both in terms of their limited availability for each student to use regularly, and in terms of the content that students access. Students track their free reading and complete quizzes for comprehension; they also use the iPads to supplement their core curriculum with fun (and sometimes unrelated) games, rather than using them to advance actual learning objectives. We are still in the process of determining access to supportive math programs, other than a piecemeal approach.

Vision for Improvement: The most important thing we need to do is rearrange our classrooms physically to allow for station setup and station rotation. We need to move away from students "owning" their desks to shared work areas that are grouped according to task. We also need to increase the number of iPads that our students can use.

Your score: ______________________________

Why?

____

____

____

____

____

____

Draft your plan

Articulate your plan for the physical and virtual environment

Review your audit results, as well as your vision for the ideal physical and virtual environment. Use the hard work you've already done in this module to draft the physical and virtual environment sections of your blended-learning plan.

For the other SMART goals you plan to tackle, use the blank sheets at the end of the workbook to draft this plan.

1. Audit the schools of implementation for your program and provide a summary of the devices, Wi-Fi access, software licenses, and facilities that are already available.

   ____

   ____

   ____

   ____

2. Provide an analysis of the ways in which your physical and virtual environment is already sufficient to deliver your intended models, and the places where you have gaps.

   ____

   ____

   ____

   ____

3. Describe your priorities for improving the physical and virtual infrastructure and space for the schools of implementation.

   ____

   ____

   ____

   ____

Before moving on, remember to self-assess your work. Look at the Physical and Virtual Environment Rubric and see how you'd score yourself. Keep working until your plan is exceptional!

APPENDIX

Our evaluation of physical and virtual environment plans

Statement 1

Our score: 9

Why? This statement provides a full summary of the formal audit report along all dimensions of hardware, software, Wi-Fi, and facilities. It showcases an accurate understanding of the ways that the existing environment already accommodates the proposed blended-learning design and the ways in which it will need to change toward a compelling new vision for the physical and virtual environment.

Statement 2

Our score: 3

This basic response provides some data about the existing environment, but it has big data gaps. It evidences some thought about issues that need to be addressed related to the physical and virtual environment, but the analysis is superficial and inaccurate. It presents a partial vision for improvement, and the alignment with the learning design, although accurate thus far, is incomplete.

Choose the Model

Key objective

- **Understand how to choose the right blended-learning model to meet the needs of specific learners and environments**

Content summary

The importance of naming your models

If you've kept up with the earlier parts of this workbook, you have designed the student and teacher experiences already. You have a vision for the improved environment you want your students to inhabit. Now let's give language to that design by naming the blended model or models that you plan to deploy to give structure to this design.

As we discussed in Module 1.1, using the vocabulary of the blended-learning models serves two purposes. First, it helps you communicate your vision to other stakeholders. When you explain that your design involves a Flipped Classroom combined with a Flex model, for example, other people who are at least basically familiar with blended learning get a preliminary idea of your intentions in only a few words. Second, naming the models helps with your research and development. Other blended programs across the world are tagging their designs with the names of the models. Enter the model name in an online search at the Blended Learning Universe or in Google, for example, and you will find examples of other blended programs that resemble your design. This can help with the research and testing that you will want to do as part of discovery-driven planning, which we discuss in Module 2.9.

This module walks you through a process to choose the best models for your needs and add that language to your blended-learning plan. By the end, you will be able to state if you are using a Station Rotation, Lab Rotation, Flipped Classroom, Individual Rotation, Flex, A La Carte, and/or Enriched Virtual and explain your reasons for that choice.

> Go to the Blended Learning Universe (*www.blendedlearning.org/directory*) to search for examples of other schools' blended programs, which you can sort by model name.

Expand your strategy skills

Choose-the-model game

In this game, you will discover which blended-learning model meets your needs in the most ways. Go through the six questions that follow and **circle** the single answer that matches your circumstances, design, and constraints the best. As you work through each question, the models will earn a variety of points. Keep a tally of these points on the Point Board.

If you have more than one SMART goal, use the pages at the back of this workbook to play this game with each project.

Point Board

Model	Point tally
Station Rotation	
Lab Rotation	
Flipped Classroom	
Individual Rotation	
Flex	
A La Carte	
Enriched Virtual	

Six questions

Question 1: What problem are you trying to solve?

A. Core problem involving mainstream students

Give one point each to Station Rotation, Lab Rotation, and Flipped Classroom.

B. Nonconsumption problem

Give one point each to Individual Rotation, Flex, A La Carte, and Enriched Virtual.

Question 2: What type of team do you need to solve the problem?

A. Functional team. The problem is a classroom-, department-, or grade-level problem only.

Give one point each to Station Rotation and Flipped Classroom.

B. Lightweight team. The problem requires coordination outside of the classroom, department, or grade-level teachers with other parts of the school.

Give one point each to Station Rotation, Lab Rotation, and Flipped Classroom.

C. Heavyweight team. The problem requires changing the architecture of the school.

Give one point each to Station Rotation and Lab Rotation.

D. Autonomous team. The problem requires a new education model entirely.

Give one point each to Individual Rotation, Flex, A La Carte, and Enriched Virtual.

Question 3: What do you want students to control?

A. Their pace and path during the online portion of the course

Give one point each to Station Rotation, Lab Rotation, and Flipped Classroom.

B. Their pace and path throughout almost all of the course

Give one point each to Individual Rotation and Flex.

C. Their pace and path throughout almost all of the course, with the flexibility to skip in-person class at times

Give one point each to A La Carte and Enriched Virtual.

Question 4: What do you want the primary role of the teacher to be?

A. Delivering face-to-face direct instruction

Give one point each to Station Rotation and Lab Rotation.

B. Providing face-to-face tutoring, coaching, and enrichment to supplement online lessons

Give one point each to Flipped Classroom, Individual Rotation, Flex, and Enriched Virtual.

C. Serving as the online teacher of record

Give one point to A La Carte.

Question 5: What physical space can you use?

A. Existing classrooms

Give one point each to Station Rotation and Flipped Classroom.

B. Existing classrooms plus a computer lab

Give one point to Lab Rotation.

C. A large, open learning space

Give one point each to Individual Rotation, Flex, and Enriched Virtual.

D. Any safe, supervised setting

Give one point to A La Carte.

Question 6: How many Internet-enabled devices are available?

A. Enough for a fraction of the students

Give one point each to Station Rotation and Lab Rotation.

B. Enough for all students throughout the entire class period

Give one point each to Station Rotation, Lab Rotation, Individual Rotation, and Flex.

C. Enough for all students to use in class and have at home or after school

Give one point to all the models.

Which model got the most points on the tally board? Write the name here:

____

Content summary

Prioritizing the questions

Points alone do not determine the best model to fit your circumstances, design, and constraints. Sometimes a single question is important enough to decide the issue. There are several reasons why some teams must give extra weight to one or more of the questions as they select the best model for their needs.

Sometimes the most important factor in choosing a model is Question 1: What problem are you trying to solve? Core problems are difficult to solve with disruptive models—the Individual Rotation, Flex, A La Carte, and Enriched Virtual models—because the performance hurdle for core problems serving mainstream students is more difficult to surmount than for nonconsumption problems. In the case of core problems, the school community will only embrace a disruptive model once it becomes superior to the best version of the traditional classroom. Matching a core problem with a disruptive model means that you are setting the bar high for how good your design and implementation need to be. In contrast, the school community is likely to embrace disruptive models for nonconsumption problems, because the alternative in these instances is nothing at all. That's a much lower bar. Bottom line: if your team is likely to face resistance from the school community, give top priority to Question 1. Match core problems to sustaining models and nonconsumption problems to disruptive models.

Other times the most important question is Question 2: What type of team do you need to solve the problem? If you are an individual teacher acting alone, your only realistic option is to form a one-person functional team. Your best bet is to implement a Flipped Classroom or simple Station Rotation, until you get more support and cover from a senior leader who can help you make the sweeping budget, staffing, scheduling, and facilities changes that the other models may require. If this is the case for you, then Question 2 is your deciding factor.

When do Questions 3 and 4 rise to the top? Question 3 asks how much you want your students to control, and Question 4 asks what you want the primary role of the teacher to be. You might choose to prioritize these questions if you are determined to bring about a specific student experience, despite any difficulties along the way. You don't care if you don't have the right team; you are ready to embrace the challenge of deploying a disruptive model for mainstream students, and you will figure out a way to get the necessary physical space and devices. You simply want leeway to implement your vision for the student experience and teacher roles, even if you have to open a new school to do it. If this is the case for you, prioritize Questions 3 and 4.

Other teams choose to prioritize Question 5: What physical space can you use? Others choose Question 6: How many Internet-enabled devices are available? These are determining factors for schools that are constrained by physical space or access to devices and that have no hope of freeing up funds to remove these constraints through creative reallocation of expenses. For example, if it's impossible for you to provide each student with an Internet-enabled device, and there is no way to rearrange the budget, then your choice of blended models is limited to the models that do not require one-to-one devices. That limitation becomes your deciding factor.

Apply the learning

Choose the model

Reflect about which of the six questions are the highest priority for you:

1. What problem are you trying to solve?
2. What type of team do you need to solve the problem?
3. What do you want students to control?
4. What do you want the primary role of the teacher to be?
5. What physical space can you use?
6. How many Internet-connected devices are available?

Circle the highest-priority question(s) and explain your choice.

____

____

____

____

____

____

With your tally from the Point Board and your reflection about the questions that are highest priority, you are ready to choose the model or combination of models for your plan. Which models got the highest points? Which are the highest priority? Combine these data points to identify the right model(s) for you. Write your answer here:

____

View rubric and benchmark

Naming your models

Your blended-learning plan will be more precise and clear if you specify the model(s) that you intend to use and explain your reasoning. Use the Choose the Model Rubric to help you develop and evaluate this section of your plan.

Choose the Model Rubric

	Exceptional 3	Advanced 2	Basic 1	Inadequate 0
Model selection	Names and justifies the **appropriate models** of blended learning as the engines to power the design, given the site's circumstances.	Names the model(s) that will be used and explains why, but the fit is **less than optimal**, given the site's circumstances.	Names the model(s) that will be used, but the fit is **questionable**, given the site's circumstances.	Names the model(s), but the choice is **unreasonable**.

Read this example of a statement about model choice that a real school team developed, followed by our evaluation of that statement according to the rubric.

Sample model-choice statement

Our small, rural district with just one high school has a focused but persistent problem: We do not have the teachers to provide language learning other than English to our students. Although our district has a strong tradition of sending students into the skilled trades and agricultural work, we need to support all our students, including those with goals to attend selective and rigorous colleges, for which foreign language study is an important preparation. We have chosen an A La Carte model as the best and most effective engine to power our blended-learning design, although it's not a perfect fit in every way. Our district's lack of foreign language learning resources presents a nonconsumption problem for us; to solve this, we will need an autonomous team. We want students to be able to choose the language they will study and then set the timing and pace of their coursework. The members of our autonomous team will work with each other, with a focus group of students, and with the teachers and librarian who will be the students' accountability partners to set the standards of the pace and amount of online content that will qualify students to receive district credit for their learning; the online tracking of content mastery within the language learning program will be used to determine course grades and additions to the students' GPA.

We have 37 devices with Internet access in the library that will be dedicated to this initiative; we estimate that about 50 students may want to participate in this initiative. The librarian will maintain the reservations for these devices, to optimize student use of them from early to extended hours of the school day and all throughout it, including lunch. Students with Internet access at home will be able to continue their progress from there. We will work hard to ensure that the standard for course credit can be achieved solely from working at school, and part of our overall plan is to expand students' access to Internet-connected devices at home. Finally, although none of our teachers speak foreign languages (other than Spanish) well enough to coach students in content, we will establish accountability partners: All students who want to take advantage of this initiative will be assigned to a teacher (in a maximum 10:1 ratio) who will meet with them weekly to check their progress, support them with general time-management and learning strategies, and encourage them toward the standards for course credit and content mastery. A few teachers have also expressed interest in co-learning with their students, which will act as a powerful example within our school of a growth mindset and the value of lifelong learning.

Scoring explanation

We score this strong statement a 3 according to the rubric. It uses the appropriate A La Carte model of blended learning to solve a persistent nonconsumption problem, and it justifies the choice convincingly. The statement is accurate in identifying the lack of a 1:1 student-to-device ratio as a potential problem, but it is thoughtful about resolving that.

Draft your plan

Articulate your statement about model choice

Now it's your turn. What blended-learning model or combination of models do you plan to implement, and why? To justify your answer, refer to the six questions listed earlier in the "Apply the learning" worksheet in this module and to your prioritization of the questions. Draft your response here.

____

____

____

____

____

____

____

____

Repeat this process for any additional SMART goals, using the blank pages at the end of this workbook.

Before finalizing your statement about model choice, review it against the Choose the Model Rubric. Don't move forward until you are convinced that your statement is exceptional.

Culture

MODULE 2.7

Key objectives

- Know how to create a new organizational culture or fix an existing culture
- Develop an action plan for establishing cultural norms to support a blended-learning implementation

Content summary

How to create and change organizational culture

No blended-learning implementation will be successful without a positive and systematic culture to support it. In fact, a team's efforts are sure to fall short if the team members fail to turn their attention to designing and creating strong cultural norms to cement their design together and make it run well.

Edgar Schein, a professor emeritus at MIT and expert in organizational behavior, defines culture in these terms:

> Culture is a way of working together toward common goals that have been followed so frequently and so successfully that people don't even think about trying to do things another way. If a culture has formed, people will autonomously do what they need to do to be successful.[1]

Good culture does not have to emerge from happenstance or luck. Leaders can deliberately build the strong culture they need by following six steps:

1. Define a problem or task that recurs again and again.
2. Appoint a group to solve the problem.
3. If the group fails, ask it to try again with a different process.
4. If it succeeds, ask the same group to repeat the process every time the problem recurs.
5. Write down and promote the culture.
6. Live in a way that is consistent with the culture.

The first step is to start by defining a problem or task—one that recurs again and again in the school, or one that you expect will arise once blended learning is in place. Next, pull a group out of the organization and appoint it to figure out how to solve the problem. Set aside the school's existing pattern of response to the problem. The idea here is to try something new that will work better.

If the group fails, that's OK. Ask it to try again with a different process. Then once the group has succeeded, don't disperse the team. Instead, ask the same team to solve the problem every time it recurs—over and over again. The more times they solve the problem the same way and find success, the more instinctive it becomes. Culture is formed through repetition. All too often when problems crop up, if a solution works, the discussion ends and the team disbands. If the solution doesn't work, the leader changes or reprimands the team. Neither of these approaches works for creating a deliberate culture.[2]

Once a culture has been shown to work, write it down and talk about it as often as possible. Many school leaders see the value in having a written artifact of their culture that they can promote. But merely writing and talking about the culture are not enough. Leaders must make decisions that are entirely aligned to it.

You can discern the health of an organization's culture by asking, "When faced with a choice on how to do something, do members of the organization make the decision that the culture 'wanted' them to make? And was the feedback they received consistent with that?"

The rules for changing a bad culture and for shaping a culture from scratch are identical. Identify and define the problems that need to be solved in the new organization and then solve them. If the solutions are successful, then repeat until the processes and priorities become reflex within the organization's culture.

Check for understanding

Diagnose what's causing the culture

Review the description of a real classroom in the following vignette. In the space provided after the vignette, note the recurring problems and tasks that the teacher faced, the processes that she used to solve the problems or complete the tasks, and the ways that she promoted and reinforced the culture.

Vignette: Ms. Weissman's classroom

During the 2015–16 school year, Rebecca Weissman taught a grades 1–2 combination class at Redwood Heights Elementary School in the Oakland Unified School District. She implemented blended learning to help her students reach academic growth goals in math and reading and to nurture their skills and dispositions related to agency and growth mindset. For math, students did a Station Rotation that included the online program ST Math, a guided group station to solve word problems, and peer collaboration. Her reading block was an Individual Rotation that included personalized, individual work (some of which was online), working with partners, and meeting with their teacher for a small-group lesson, a one-on-one conference, a one-on-one reading session, or an assessment.

Ms. Weissman needed uninterrupted time during each math and reading block to give select students her full attention. She purchased a hair wreath made of green ivy, which she called her "off-limits crown," and taught the students that when she wore it, they should avoid interrupting her as she was focusing on an individual student or group. She also taught the students to request that the online-assessment service Literably evaluate their progress when they felt they were ready for the next level of books to read. That allowed students to level up on their own without interrupting her one-on-ones.

Each day, students hit roadblocks, had questions, and needed support. Ms. Weissman needed a way to empower them to solve their own problems to the extent possible. She developed a goal-tracker worksheet that the students completed each morning to identify the progress that they planned to make during independent time. She did read-alouds of books about agency and growth mindset, such as *My Name Is Not Isabella* and *The Fantastic Elastic Brain.* She posted and discussed mantras such as "Mistakes are wonderful opportunities to learn" and "The only true failure can come if you quit." Throughout the day, Ms. Weissman made efforts to praise students who showed responsibility for their progress, who overcame obstacles, or who requested the support they needed. She also set up a Mindset Box, where students could deposit slips of paper with notes about classmates they observed showing agency and growth mindset. She pulled out a slip or two each day, read the praise aloud, and gave the notes to the students whom she had praised so that they could share them with their parents.

Reflection questions

Answers to these questions are included in the appendix at the end of this module.

1. What are Ms. Weissman's priorities for her classroom?

   ___

   ___

2. What are some of the problems and tasks that recurred again and again in this classroom?

   ___

   ___

3. What processes did Ms. Weissman establish to solve the problems or complete the tasks in order to accomplish her priorities?

   ___

   ___

   ___

   ___

   ___

   ___

4. What types of feedback promoted and reinforced the culture?

   ___

   ___

Expand your strategy skills

Practice brainstorming solutions

Imagine that you are on an autonomous team that's in charge of designing and implementing a blended-learning plan, including creating a strong culture to help the program thrive. Your team has identified several tasks and problems that will recur again and again as the program gets under way. Now it's time to think of ways to solve the problems and complete the tasks.

For each of the following hypothetical problems or tasks, brainstorm one possible process or routine that you could pilot-test to see if it works. Keep in mind that your team will need to promote and live by this method, if it proves successful, to deeply embed it into your organizational culture.

Recurring problem or task	Possible process or routine for resolving it
Each week, one or two students transfer into your high school. Most come from traditional environments. You need an efficient way to onboard them into an environment where they set their own goals, do half of their learning independently, and meet in a large, open learning space.	
Your faculty includes one expert mathematician, one published writer, one noted historian, and one accomplished scientist, in addition to several counselors and social workers. The subject-matter experts have enough time to meet with each student for 15 minutes twice per week for individual tutoring. They want to effectively use this time and provide the right help at that given moment for each student. That will require up-to-the-moment data about students' progress.	

Recurring problem or task	Possible process or routine for resolving it
Your program seeks to empower students to control their own learning, take responsibility, and find joy in seeing that they can make progress each day. You anticipate that the large, open learning space could get noisy and unruly under this system. You will need a way of maintaining order that is consistent with your values of student-driven learning and joy in learning.	

View rubric and benchmarks

Developing a successful culture

Now let's start thinking about the elements of culture that will be important for your own blended-learning plan.

For the purposes of this plan, you do not need to design every single aspect of your culture. Instead, use the plan to show your competency in the process of creating culture by identifying three to four problems or tasks that will recur again and again in your blended program and your best ideas for resolving them. Later, as you get deeper into implementation, you will want to take the time to develop a complete list of all the critical elements of the culture that you will need to create.

Use the Culture Rubric to help you start to develop the culture for your program. It describes the things that distinguish an exceptional vision for culture (3) from one that is advanced (2), basic (1), or inadequate (0).

Culture Rubric

	Exceptional 3	Advanced 2	Basic 1	Inadequate 0
List of problems or tasks	Provides a list of **3–4 high-priority problems or tasks** that will recur or are likely to arise in a student-centered blended-learning environment.	Provides a list, although the problems or tasks are **not the highest priority** in this kind of environment.	Provides **only 1–2 high-priority problems or tasks;** other problems/tasks are low priority.	Evidences a **lack of understanding** about what a recurring problem or task is in this kind of environment.
Proposed routines	Proposes routines aligned to the problem/task that are **all** of the following: efficient, student driven, and sustainable over time.	Proposes routines aligned to the problem/task that are **most** of the following: efficient, student driven, and sustainable over time.	Proposes routines, but they **do meet the criteria** to be successful.	Routines are **not aligned** to the problem/task.

	Exceptional 3	Advanced 2	Basic 1	Inadequate 0
Promotion	Proposes a plan for promoting the new processes until they become **planted deeply into the culture** across the system.	Proposes a plan for promoting the new processes, but it is **less than comprehensive.**	Describes how the team will promote the process, but it is **superficial or unlikely to work.**	**Skips** the important step of promoting the culture.

To give you a sense of how to apply this rubric, the following is an excerpt of a culture plan that a real team developed, followed by our evaluation of that culture plan according to the rubric.

Sample culture plan

We will address three challenges that will arise as we move forward with our plan: securing family and community buy-in, ensuring student ownership of learning and progress monitoring, and teacher mastery of small-group and differentiated instruction.

Family and community buy-in

Our school already has a strong culture of involving parents in critical aspects of their child's education. Parents are extremely involved and work with teachers to support students through their journeys, and teachers appreciate and welcome the level of parental involvement. We will extend this culture of support to blended learning as well. Families will support students as they complete online, adaptive homework, and parents will check online data to monitor their child's progress. As part of the Flipped Classroom model, students will have to work independently at home, and parent support in this will be vital to success.

Strategies include:

- Parents will commit to: (1) encourage their student to complete work independently and (2) do everything possible to have someone at home available for help as needed.

- Host quarterly parent workshops to educate parents and the community on technology, curriculum, and how best to help their students.
- Incentivize teacher participation in parent workshops and use the Parent Teacher Association to make workshops part of our culture.
- Make the parent workshops fun and social to build parent engagement with teachers and school administration.
- Digital and information literacy and safety will be a key focus area that addresses parent concerns.
- Blended-learning data will be part of student report cards and discussed in conferences.

Student ownership of learning and progress monitoring

Having students set and track progress on their own goals is integral to the blended-learning model; it allows students to take ownership of learning, control their pace, reflect on their strengths and challenges, and become intrinsically motivated to learn. Students will learn how to access their progress data on the online software, exit tickets, and other formative assessments and make connections with their NWEA MAP scores.

- Students will set short-term (weekly) and long-term (semester) goals for successful lesson completion and target standards.
- Students will maintain a journal of goals, progress, and reflections.
- Teachers will bring joy around meeting goals and facilitate student planning of celebrations.
- Goal setting and progress will become a major part of class (with students leading celebrations) and of parent conferences and report card night.

Teacher mastery of small-group and individual coaching

- Teachers will use formative assessments and data collected by adaptive digital software to inform flexible small grouping.

- Teachers will establish a routine of meeting individually with each student for 30 minutes each week to provide feedback and mentoring.
- Content teams will meet twice weekly, and part of the meeting will be allocated to managing and improving flexible ability groupings.
- Teachers peer-coach each other to provide each other with observations and feedback.

As our model scales, pilot school teachers and staff will serve as coaches and models for their peers across our district. Established schools can model their parent workshops, student routines, goal setting, and small-group/individual routines.

Scoring explanation

We score this plan a total of 8. It earns 3 points for its thoughtful list of three high-priority problems and tasks that will recur again and again during the program. It earns another 3 points for the thoughtful list of new routines; it proposes reasonable and sustainable routines and processes for completing each of the tasks successfully. Finally, it earns 2 points for its plans to reinforce culture. It has stated clearly how the district hopes to promote the cultural processes initially, but it is incomplete about reinforcing and establishing the culture over time through ongoing celebration of those who are living the culture.

Practice evaluating

Score these plans for creating culture

Rate the following culture plans on a 0–3 scale using the Culture Rubric. Explain your reasons why. Our answers are in the appendix at the end of this module.

Statement 1

Our district considers three issues as critically important for developing the culture needed to foster and support personalized learning. These areas will be addressed through the establishment of routines and processes designed to instill the new processes within the participating schools and ultimately across the entire district:

1. **Family and community engagement**—Engaging parents and the community in the planning, implementation, and evaluation processes involved with our blended-learning pilot program
2. **Data-based decision making**—Developing a data-driven school culture that prompts teachers and students to use student achievement data routinely to support continuous improvement
3. **Cultural norms**—Establishing norms for students and teachers specific for personalized-learning environments, including norms for collaboration, improvement within and across iterations, and scalability

Routines and processes for gaining family and community buy-in and engagement

- **Communicate and educate**—We will provide guidance and support as we educate parents on how to support their students differently, how to ask the right questions, and how to monitor progress via the online student dashboard. To do this, we will provide ongoing parent/student informational meetings to introduce the blended-learning pilot program. To ensure that *parents* feel heard and have their concerns addressed, we will have grade-level teams and administrators available to meet in small-group coffee chats to explain the program and how it is different from a traditional classroom. We will host parent, student, and teacher conferences at least once per six weeks, and students will lead parent/teacher conferences by Year 2 to demonstrate how they are driving their own learning. We will introduce parents to the online dashboard, which will allow them to view student academic performance and progress. Their feedback is important to help us continually improve our model. We will also conduct student and parent focus groups and surveys throughout the year.
- **Showcase**—Parent emails, including program updates and showcases of class work, will be sent out weekly. We will make these proof-of-concept classrooms available for observations by district staff to spread the successes and enthusiasm for the program organically. We will

present the success of the project in district-wide meetings, with our education council, all our campus administrators, and school board.

- **Engage campus- and network-level support staff**—Our district has a wealth of instructional and technical staff who are ready to support personalized learning. We will train teachers and administrators as well as other key players, including instructional technology specialists, curriculum specialists, campus peer facilitators, and campus content specialists. This engagement will provide teachers with needed technology and curriculum support and promote a culture of involvement, engagement, and collaboration. As the program scales, we will morph instructional technology, campus content specialist, and peer facilitator duties to support the pilot program.

Routines and processes for data-driven decision making

Through extensive and ongoing staff development, we will train staff on how to collect, analyze, disaggregate, and use data to drive student achievement. We will set clear expectations for data use and embed these expectations into our professional development and professional-learning communities. A minimum of one weekly team meeting will be dedicated to student "data talk," meaning discussion about each student's results. We will provide a data dashboard to give students, teachers, and parents instant access to real-time assessment data. This data allows students to have agency over the choice of content and the pace of learning. Real-time assessment data will guide them to make calculated decisions of what objectives need to be mastered and select the content that best meets their needs to accomplish their goals.

Routines and processes for establishing cultural norms within and across pilots

We will conduct weekly two-question surveys of parents, students, and staff and post results for everyone to see. Each district-wide meeting, we will have campus leaders share one thing that they did that month to break free from a process or mindset that was preventing needed innovations. Pilot classrooms will be available for tours for stakeholders who are interested in learning more about blended learning.

We will promote all of the above routines and processes to establish them in the culture through three strategies:

- We will write down and post every new process on a wall chart in the entryway to each campus.
- At monthly district-wide meetings, we will do shout-outs of teachers and leaders who are living by these norms.
- We will model the processes and routines in the way that we do professional development.

Your score: ______________________________

Why?

____

____

____

____

____

____

Statement 2

Successful implementation of the pilot requires a consistent, ongoing process to establish a strong culture that holds everything in place. The three challenges with the highest priority are listed below, along with the methods to address each challenge.

1. **Collaboration time for cohort teachers**—Scheduling blocks of time for collaboration, professional development, and coaching is critical for helping teachers learn to release control to students. A full day will be provided each six weeks for cohort teachers to focus on student-centered learning through examining student needs, integrating objectives with real-world experiences, designing personalized pathways, and raising the level of engagement in learning. In addition, the weekly professional learning community (PLC) meetings will allow for continuous dialogue centered on customizing instruction with innovative, integrated practice.

2. **On-demand teacher support and training**—To guarantee the success in facilitating a blended-learning environment, teachers must transition from a teacher-directed classroom to designing personalized learning pathways to inspire student-driven learning. This shift in focus can be accomplished through the use of the online technology-enabled tools and professional development sessions customized based upon teacher goals and desired skill set for flexible, interactive, "just in time" training. The assigned Blended Learning Coach can model in the classroom, answer questions, troubleshoot problems, supply immediate feedback to teachers, and coach them using a reflective, cognitive approach. A playlist of technological resources to assist with the delivery of content and to support a student-centered learning environment will be available along with micro-credentialing and badging opportunities within the levels of professional development.

3. **Structure, routines, and procedures for blended learning**—Functional and vertical PLC teams will meet regularly to sequence instruction and create procedures and routines based upon research-based effective practice. Teachers will model for students to ensure a smooth transition, and then students will assume responsibility for their learning. Training the students to take ownership of their individualized learning is vital to success. Teachers

will outline, teach, and consistently reinforce student expectations. Students will ultimately become more independent in their learning as teachers serve as facilitators of student learning. Support systems will be embedded in the blended-learning cycle as students own their progress within a competency-based mastery structure.

Your score: ______________________

Why?

____

____

____

____

____

____

Statement 3

Making the transition between areas of study is the most problematic task for our students; inefficient transitions can waste valuable learning or productive socializing time. We are proposing a routine where our students will check in with a time-tracking system to mark their end times on their last project and their start times on the next one; even by measuring the lapses between the two, students will waste less time. We will also require them to note in the time-tracking system what occupied their attention between tasks. We will assign a team to promote the time tracking and to evaluate and report on the data it contains.

Your score: ______________________

Why?

____

____

____

____

____

____

Draft your plan

Articulate your plan for creating culture

If you've made it this far in the workbook, your blended-learning plan is really taking shape. But it's missing the glue that holds everything together if it fails to address the plan for creating a strong and lasting culture.

Take the time to think deeply before completing the table here to draft your culture plans.

For the other SMART goals you plan to tackle, use the blank sheets at the end of the workbook to draft your culture plan.

1. List three to four recurring problems or tasks that are the most important for students, teachers, and/or administrators to resolve day by day during your program.
2. For each of the high-priority, recurring tasks or problems you listed, identify a process or routine that could work to resolve it successfully.
3. Describe how the team will promote this process or routine to deeply plant it into the culture across the system.

You may complete this activity by using the table here.

Recurring problem or task	Possible process or routine for resolving it	How team will promote the culture

Use this space as a parking lot to note other recurring tasks or problems that are lower priority but that you still want to be sure to address during implementation.

- ____
- ____
- ____
- ____
- ____
- ____
- ____
- ____
- ____
- ____

Before moving on, remember to self-assess your work. Look at the Culture Rubric to decide how you'd score yourself.

APPENDIX

Check for understanding: Diagnose what's causing the culture

1. Ms. Weissman's priorities were for her students to reach academic growth goals in math and reading and to improve their skills and dispositions related to agency and growth mindset.
2. Ms. Weissman needed uninterrupted time during each math and reading block to give select students her full attention. She also needed a way to empower students to solve their own problems to the extent possible so that they developed the skill of agency and so that she could conduct her individual and small-group meetings.
3. She used the off-limits crown, trained her students to request Literably assessments when they were ready, implemented a student-driven goal-tracking system, did read-alouds of books that reinforced the mind-sets she wanted to nurture, and discussed and posted mantras.
4. Ms. Weissman used intentional language to acknowledge the students who exemplified the culture she wanted to create. Also, she used the Mindset Box to encourage students to recognize and praise others who were living the culture.

Our evaluation of plans for creating culture

Statement 1

Our score: 9

This is a strong statement for creating culture. We give a score of 3 to the thoughtful list of three high-priority problems or tasks that will recur again and again during the program. It proposes reasonable routines or processes for completing each of the tasks successfully; we score this segment a 3. It also proposes a sound plan for promoting the new processes until they become planted deeply into the culture across the system, from defining the problem or task, to appointing a group to solve that problem, to iterating that process, to repeating successful solutions, to writing down and promoting the solutions, and finally to moving forward with consistency and integrity. We score its reinforcement of culture a 3.

Statement 2

Our score: 5

We rate the list of problems or tasks for this plan a 2; the plan provides the required list in all respects, but the first two problems or tasks are not the highest priority in a student-centered blended-learning environment, and they are repetitive of each other. Although this plan proposes routines or processes, they could be much more student driven to model students working together to create their own norms; we rate this segment a 2. This plan somewhat describes how the team will promote the process, but in failing to detail how they will reinforce the culture, it is mostly incomplete or problematic. We score this last segment a 1.

Statement 3

Our score: 3

We score this basic plan a 1 for its list of problems or tasks because it mentions only one problem and causes the reader to wonder whether the problem to solve is sloppy transitions or, more fundamentally, an instructional design that causes students to disengage and dawdle. It proposes a new routine that in itself could be cumbersome and time-consuming; we score this segment a 1. Although it describes somewhat how the team will promote the process, the plan is mostly incomplete and problematic for how it focuses on what the team is trying to eliminate (wasted time) rather than what it is trying to create and promote (effective use of time). We score this plan's reinforcement of culture a 1.

Notes

1. Edgar Schein, *Organizational Culture and Leadership* (San Francisco: Jossey-Bass Publishers, 1988).

2. Clayton M. Christensen, Karen Dillon, and James Allworth, *How Will You Measure Your Life?* (New York: HarperCollins, 2012), 164.

Budget

Key objectives

- ○ Understand the difference between one-time and recurring costs, revenue, and savings
- ○ Model out the budget for your blended-learning plan
- ○ Craft a narrative that shows a full understanding of the levers you are using to turn your blended design into a reality

Content summary

Building the budget

With your design in place and a plan to create a strong culture, the next topic is everyone's favorite: the budget. Do you have the money to make your dream design a reality?

A coy way to ask this same question might be: Can you afford *not* to make your design a reality? Either way, figuring out your budget—on what you need to spend and how often, where you can save money, and from where extra dollars will come—is critical.

We did not address this topic in *Blended* other than to write of its importance and talk about how blended learning could help control costs. As we have traveled around the country and worked with school teams designing and implementing blended designs, however, we have seen that the topic deserves a more in-depth treatment.

To be clear, we don't expect you to become a finance whiz just from working through this module. We recommend working with the business manager in your school or other appropriate finance person to get the budget right and make sure your project will be sustainable. We also recommend learning from organizations like Afton Partners (http://www.aftonpartners.com/), which exists to help schools develop financially sustainable models. But we also want you to be able to think about the core financial drivers of your blended model and where you may need to get creative to make it work so that you can deliver on your SMART goal and see the model live on for years to come. When you are stretching the budget for blended learning, creativity is the key to success.

Sustainability

As you construct your budget, it is important that you do so with an eye toward the future. That means planning for something that will be sustainable year after year. Some schools are able to secure grant funding to help implement the first wave of blended learning—a big help to be sure. But for the innovation to be sustainable over time, the schools must find a way to keep their programs alive after one-time grant dollars are spent and to continue to invest to bring the programs to full scale.

One time versus recurring

As we work through the budget, we will look at both the costs and revenue. We will also map out which costs and revenue occur just one time up-front as opposed to those that recur year after year. Balancing costs and revenue—or creating a bit of a surplus—is what yields sustainability.

Understanding which costs and revenue or savings are one-time rather than ongoing is critical to building your model successfully. For example, although buying devices might seem like a one-time cost, the reality is that you'll have to refresh them over time—every three to five years—to stay up with the latest technology as well as when devices break. As a result, there is both a one-time, up-front cost and a smaller, recurring cost.

Check for understanding

Distinguish between one-time and recurring costs

Next to each item, write down whether it represents a one-time or recurring cost.

1. Initial purchase of one $250 Chromebook for every three students ____________
2. Savings of $5 per student in printed materials ____________
3. Refreshing one-third of laptops every year ____________
4. Cost of $10 per student in annual software licenses ____________
5. Receipt of a $10,000 grant from the district parents' fund ____________
6. Additional $7,000 in revenue from moving from 27:1 student-to-teacher ratio to 28:1 ____________
7. Initial purchase of one set of headphones for every student ____________
8. Refreshing one-third of headphones every year ____________
9. Cost of a one-time multiday workshop for teachers and staff introducing blended learning ____________
10. Retrofitting of classrooms—by adding electrical sockets, appropriate furniture, and so forth—to be ready for blended learning ____________

Expand your strategy skills

Calculate the budget impact

Let's dive one step deeper to estimate the costs, revenue, and savings in some of the line items from the previous activity.

1. If there are thirty students in a class and we purchase one $250 Chromebook for every three students, the total up-front cost will be ______________________

2. If we save $5 per student from not having to print certain materials anymore over the course of a year, in a class of thirty students, the recurring savings is ______________

3. If we refresh one-third of laptops every year in a class where we have ten laptops that each cost $250, the recurring cost will be roughly ______________________

4. If we spend $10 per student in annual software licenses for a class of thirty, the total cost is

   ____

5. If we assume that the scenarios in Questions 1 through 4 all take place, how much money will we spend in Year 1? ______________________

   What about in Year 2? ______________________

6. If we assume that the scenarios in Questions 1 through 4 all take place *and* that we move from a student-to-teacher ratio of 27:1 to one of 28:1 and bring in an additional $7,000 per year per classroom, in the first year, how much money do we effectively bring in when considering savings and additional revenue in Year 1?

   ____

   ____

   What about in Year 2? ______________________

7. If we combine the scenarios in Questions 5 and 6, can we afford to implement our blended design? Explain why.

   ____

   ____

Draft your plan

Costs

If your blended-learning design is for just one classroom, then you have a few items to cost out: software, hardware, and infrastructure—from your Internet connectivity to your electrical outlets or charging stations and furniture needs.

If you are focused at a school or district level, you have a few more costs to consider, including staffing, professional development, other facilities costs, software licenses for the district, and administrative overhead.

The good news is that in the course of this workbook, you have already thought through and listed out most of these items, so you just need to take that list, figure out which cost items are one-time and which are recurring, and plug in appropriate dollar amounts. If you are not sure whether something has a recurring cost or what a dollar amount should be, ask the appropriate person on your team or in your school for assistance.

First, we'll brainstorm one-time expenses, followed by recurring ones. In the charts that follow, we break out school investments versus district or school network investments to help you capture all of the costs. Remember to include staff, professional development, mentoring, time and scheduling, facilities, and anything else you may need to ensure the success of your initiative. District-level investments might include things like training central staff, procuring an LMS for the district, or creating an office or position to support multiple schools. Finally, at the end we add up the year-by-year one-time, recurring, school-level, and district-level costs to capture the full budgetary impact. We've provided some examples to give you an idea of how you can do this. Remember to sequence the investments so that they align with your implementation plans.

You can draft your budget here in the workbook—or we've also provided a way for you to complete the audit using Google Sheets.

To use Google Sheets, go to http://bit.ly/BlendedBudgetTable and click on the "Make a copy" icon. A new page will open with your own copy of the budgeting tables that we use in this workbook.

Also, for your other SMART goals, we have provided these charts and templates at the end of the book. Fill them out there, and use the blank sheets for your budget narrative, which we explain toward the end of the module.

School-Level Costs									
One-Time Expenses									
Cost Item	**Per-Unit Cost ($)**	**No. of Units**	**Subtotal ($)**	**Year 1**	**Year 2**	**Year 3**	**Year 4**	**Year 5**	**Notes**
Example: Chromebooks	250	10	2,500	2,500					
Total School-Level One-Time Expenses									
Recurring Expenses									
Cost Item	**Per-Unit Cost ($)**	**No. of Units**	**Subtotal ($)**	**Year 1**	**Year 2**	**Year 3**	**Year 4**	**Year 5**	**Notes**
Example: Chromebook refresh	250	3	750	—	—	750	750	750	
Total School-Level Recurring Expenses									

Central Costs									
One-Time Expenses									
Cost Item	**Per-Unit Cost ($)**	**No. of Units**	**Subtotal ($)**	**Year 1**	**Year 2**	**Year 3**	**Year 4**	**Year 5**	**Notes**
Example: District PD/ conference	50,000	1	50,000	50,000					
Total Central One-Time Expenses									
Recurring Expenses									
Cost Item	**Per-Unit Cost ($)**	**No. of Units**	**Subtotal ($)**	**Year 1**	**Year 2**	**Year 3**	**Year 4**	**Year 5**	**Notes**
Example: LMS license	10	2,500	25,000	12,500	25,000	25,000	25,000	25,000	We roll this out to only half of district in Year 1; therefore, we don't incur full cost until Year 2.

Recurring Expenses									
Cost Item	Per-Unit Cost ($)	No. of Units	Subtotal ($)	Year 1	Year 2	Year 3	Year 4	Year 5	Notes
Total Central Recurring Expenses									

Total School-Level and Central Costs						
	Year 1	Year 2	Year 3	Year 4	Year 5	Total
TOTAL Expenses (One-Time and Recurring)						

Draft your plan

Revenue and savings

Now it is time to think through what incremental revenue you can bring in or savings you can realize so that you can afford the yearly costs.

We have already illustrated some of the funding you might capture to make your design a reality. Grants and philanthropic funds can often bring in valuable one-time funds to kick-start an implementation. Savings from not buying certain books or printing out certain worksheets or from changing your staffing ratios may allow you to make an initiative sustainable for the long haul.

Often, implementing a plan of this magnitude comes down to trade-offs: Is having a 28:1 student-to-teacher ratio with plenty of devices worth it compared to having a 27:1 student-to-teacher ratio with no devices? Is a program that you have always run worth continuing, or is it something that maybe has outlived its utility, and the funds would be better spent supporting this blended initiative? These can be difficult questions to consider, which is why having a team with which to debate them can be so important.

With that in mind, it's time to dig in. In the following tables, we first capture one-time incremental funds. (They of course could be received over a few years—for example, a three-year, $75,000 grant.) Then we capture recurring revenue and recurring savings from activities you stop doing and from which you can reallocate the funding.

Funding							
Incremental Funding							
Item	**Year 1**	**Year 2**	**Year 3**	**Year 4**	**Year 5**	**Total**	**Notes**
Example: Philanthropic grant	20,000	20,000	20,000			60,000	
Total Incremental Funding							

Recurring Revenue and Savings							
Item	**Year 1**	**Year 2**	**Year 3**	**Year 4**	**Year 5**	**Total**	**Notes**
Example: Printing savings	150	300	500	500	500	1,950	There is a ramp-up until we realize full savings
Total Reallocation of Funds							

	Year 1	Year 2	Year 3	Year 4	Year 5	Total	Notes
TOTAL Funds Available							

Draft your plan

Full budget

Now put the line items from the Total Funds Available and Total Expenses tables into the following chart to calculate your year-by-year and total surpluses or deficits. This will help you see whether your plan is realistic and where you may need to make changes. Feel free to adjust until you have a budget that is realistic and that makes your blended design affordable.

Full Budget

	Year 1	Year 2	Year 3	Year 4	Year 5	Total
TOTAL Funds Available						
TOTAL Expenses						
TOTAL Surplus (Deficit)						

Content summary

Crafting the budget narrative

As a final step and a check to make sure your budget makes sense and is realistic—and that you have a good grasp of how all the parts interact with each other—writing a brief budget narrative is useful. The budget narrative should capture how your district will fund the critical investments required for the success of your plan and how you will acquire the funds needed to implement successfully over the relevant time period. If, at this stage, your budget plan does not feel realistic, consider revising other parts of your plan to make it so, or brainstorming creative ways to make the budget work. Module 2.9, Discovery-Driven Planning, will also offer a systematic way to make tweaks and fundamental changes to your plan.

View rubric and benchmarks

Sizing up the budget narrative

The following Budget Narrative Rubric distinguishes an inadequate budget narrative (0) from a basic one (1), advanced (2), and exceptional (3).

Budget Narrative Rubric

	Exceptional 3	Advanced 2	Basic 1	Inadequate 0
Sources/Uses of funds	Provides a **complete** narrative of key one-time and recurring sources and uses of funds required over a five-year time frame. These sources of funds may include "internally generated" resource reallocation or partnership opportunities.	Provides a mostly comprehensive narrative of sources and uses of funds, but may be **missing a few key costs/ revenues**.	Provides a partial narrative of sources and uses of funds, but **does not include many of the likely one-time and recurring costs/ revenues**.	Provides **no specifics** as to use of funds or revenue sources to fund the initiative.

Budget Narrative Rubric

	Exceptional 3	Advanced 2	Basic 1	Inadequate 0
Sustainability	Articulates a plan for how the district or school intends to **sustain operational changes** necessary after incremental, one-time funding has been exhausted.	Discusses sustainability, but the plan **may lead to minor budget deficits later in implementation**.	Discusses sustainability, but the plan **will likely lead to minor budget deficits**.	Does **not address sustainability OR** assumes that grant funding will continue to make the initiative work on an ongoing basis.
Creativity	Identifies opportunities to fund and scale **creatively** through cost-saving efforts, partnerships, in-kind services, or other solutions to help scale successfully with limited incremental funding in the long term.	Identifies opportunities to fund and scale that show a modest effort to think creatively, but **one to two ideas may be unrealistic or overlooked**.	Presents an idea or two to fund and scale creatively, but **does not evidence the kind of creativity that will lead to an actual ability to pull off the plan** with limited incremental funding in the long term.	Presents **no creative sources of revenue or savings**.
Table	Supports narrative with a simple spreadsheet or table that includes costs and revenue for a five-year planning period. The numbers match the narrative.	Provides a spreadsheet or table of costs and revenue for a five-year planning period that is **mostly aligned to the narrative**.	Provides a spreadsheet or table, but the **numbers in it are not aligned to the narrative** and/or there are **major gaps** or inaccuracies.	Table is **incomplete OR** does not create a balanced budget or one with a surplus.

Read through this example of a budget narrative that a real school team developed, followed by our evaluation of that statement according to the rubric. We have also included a snapshot of their spreadsheet to give you the numbers from which the narrative was crafted. As you read the narrative and before reading our evaluation, see if you can spot the plan's strengths and weaknesses, as it is certainly not perfect.

Sample budget narrative

Key elements of our district's blended-learning plan include purchasing a learning management system; establishing a comprehensive process for purchasing and refreshing devices; and involving teachers at the selection and training points. The following costs are critical to our plan:

- Professional development
- Learning management system (LMS)
- Infrastructure upgrades, including Internet upgrades
- Personnel costs, including project manager, extra duty stipends, training
- Retrofitting of existing campuses, including furniture upgrades
- Device procurement and refresh plan

The one-time investments that we anticipate include campus retrofitting, furniture to accommodate the new environment, device procurement for pilot campuses, Wi-Fi expansion and fiber installation, and the purchase of an LMS. We have received estimates from two LMS companies, which we used to generate projected costs for the LMS. These costs reflect the initial proprietary purchase of the system and a setup fee for Year 1.

The recurring costs we anticipate include device refresh plan, extra duty or stipend pay, substitute costs, professional support for technology and digital learning, and professional development and associated training costs. Additionally, there are recurring costs for the annual subscription for the LMS based on student population, reflecting a 2 percent growth each year over the five-year period. These estimates also reflect training costs for the LMS.

Last year, citizens approved a $200 million bond, which included $20 million for technology devices and infrastructure.

Of that $20 million, $5 million will be used for this initiative. District policy and practice dictate that debt amortization aligns with the useful life of the technology devices purchased. Along with the expansion of our network capabilities, the bond funds will facilitate the implementation of the long-range blended-learning plan by allowing the district to address new facility design and construction and retrofitting of existing campuses.

Local district funds will cover ongoing costs such as extra duty pay and substitute teacher costs, professional development, digital learning support, ongoing training costs, and the annual fees and maintenance support for the LMS.

Grant funds will cover the cost of the project manager and support and the initial purchase of the LMS. The district will assume the ongoing cost of the project manager during Year 3.

We do not anticipate significant savings from this initiative.

The district is committed to blended learning. Future budget decisions will reflect this commitment.

School-Level Costs									
One-Time Expenses									
Cost Item	Per-Unit Cost ($)	No. of Units	Subtotal ($)	Year 1	Year 2	Year 3	Year 4	Year 5	Notes
Campus retrofitting			1,000,000	600,000		400,000			
Furniture			300,000	100,000	100,000	100,000			
Wi-Fi expansion			100,000	100,000					
Fiber installation			1,500,000		1,500,000				
Total School-Level One-Time Expenses			**2,900,000**	**800,000**	**1,600,000**	**500,000**			

Recurring Expenses									
Cost Item	**Per-Unit Cost ($)**	**No. of Units**	**Subtotal ($)**	**Year1**	**Year 2**	**Year 3**	**Year 4**	**Year 5**	**Notes**
Devices	300	5,000	1,500,000	60,000	150,000	720,000	285,000	285,000	Paid from bond funds
Stipends			250,000	50,000	100,000	50,000	25,000	25,000	
Substitute costs			75,000	10,000	25,000	25,000	10,000	5,000	
Tech support			220,000	30,000	50,000	60,000	40,000	40,000	
Professional development			150,000	25,000	25,000	50,000	30,000	20,000	
Total School-Level Recurring Expenses			**2,195,000**	**175,000**	**350,000**	**905,000**	**390,000**	**375,000**	

Central Costs									
One-Time Expenses									
Cost Item	**Per-Unit Cost ($)**	**No. of Units**	**Subtotal ($)**	**Year 1**	**Year 2**	**Year 3**	**Year 4**	**Year 5**	**Notes**
LMS			25,000	25,000					
Total Central One-Time Expenses			25,000	25,000					
Recurring Expenses									
Cost Item	**Per-Unit Cost ($)**	**No. of Units**	**Subtotal ($)**	**Year 1**	**Year 2**	**Year 3**	**Year 4**	**Year 5**	**Notes**
LMS fees/ maintenance			400,000	60,000	70,000	90,000	90,000	90,000	
Project mgr			700,000	130,000	135,000	140,000	145,000	150,000	
Total Central Recurring Expenses			**1,100,000**	**190,000**	**205,000**	**230,000**	**235,000**	**240,000**	

Total School-Level and Central Costs						
	Year 1	Year 2	Year 3	Year 4	Year 5	Total
TOTAL Expenses (One-Time and Recurring)	**1,190,000**	**2,155,000**	**1,635,000**	**625,000**	**615,000**	**6,220,000**

Funding							
Incremental Funding							
Item	Year 1	Year 2	Year 3	Year 4	Year 5	Total	Notes
Grant	150,000	150,000	150,000			450,000	
District bond funds	1,000,000	2,000,000	1,000,000			5,000,000	
Total Incremental Funding	1,150,000	2,150,000	1,150,000			5,450,000	
Recurring Revenue and Savings							
Item	Year 1	Year 2	Year 3	Year 4	Year 5	Total	Notes
District reallocation of funds for salaries, training, maintenance	200,000	150,000	300,000	600,000	600,000	1,850,000	
Total Reallocation of Funds	200,000	150,000	300,000	600,000	600,000	1,850,000	

	Year 1	Year 2	Year 3	Year 4	Year 5	Total	Notes
TOTAL Funds Available	1,350,000	2,300,000	1,450,000	600,000	600,000	6,300,000	

Full Budget

	Year 1	Year 2	Year 3	Year 4	Year 5	Total
TOTAL Funds Available	1,350,000	2,300,000	1,450,000	600,000	600,000	6,300,000
TOTAL Expenses	1,190,000	2,155,000	1,635,000	625,000	615,000	6,220,000
TOTAL Surplus (Deficit)	160,000	145,000	(185,000)	(25,000)	(15,000)	80,000

Scoring explanation

We give this budget narrative 9 points out of a possible 12. It provides a complete narrative of key one-time and recurring sources and uses of funds over the full time frame. The plan is sustainable over the five years. In the absence of any savings outside of the reallocation, however, the minor budget deficits it runs in the latter years of the plan raise a concern as to what will happen after Year 5. The plan does not showcase real creativity around how to fund and scale this over the longer term, so it earns only 1 point there. In particular, relying on one-time bond funds can be a great way to jump-start a program, but it is not sufficient as a way to keep the program going at scale. Moving hardware expenditures into the operating budget as opposed to the capital budget or finding cost savings from moving to the blended-learning program can be critical ways to create a sustainable plan. The narrative does support its tables.

Draft your plan

Budget narrative

Now it's your turn to draft your own budget narrative.

Before moving on, remember to self-assess your work. Look at the Budget Narrative Rubric and see how you'd score yourself.

APPENDIX

Check for understanding: Distinguish between one-time and recurring costs

1. Once
2. Recurring
3. Recurring
4. Recurring
5. Once
6. Recurring
7. Once
8. Recurring
9. Once
10. Once

Expand your strategy skills: Calculate the budget impact

1. If there are thirty students in a class and we purchase one $250 Chromebook for every three students, the total up-front cost will be *$2,500.*
2. If we save $5 per student from not having to print certain materials anymore over the course of a year, in a class of thirty students, the recurring savings is *$150.*
3. If we refresh one-third of laptops every year in a class where we have ten laptops that each cost $250, the recurring cost will be roughly *$825.*

4. If we spend $10 per student in annual software licenses for a class of thirty, the total cost is *$300.*

5. If we assume that the scenarios in Questions 1 through 4 all take place, how much money will we spend in Year 1? *$2,800.*

   What about in Year 2? *$1,125.*

6. If we assume that the scenarios in Questions 1 through 4 all take place *and* that we move from a student-to-teacher ratio of 27:1 to one of 28:1 and bring in an additional $7,000 per year per classroom, in the first year, how much money do we effectively bring in when considering savings and additional revenue in Year 1? *$7,150.*

   What about in Year 2? *$7,150.*

7. If we combine the scenarios in Questions 5 and 6, can we afford to implement our blended design?

Yes. $7,150 minus $2,800 equals a surplus of $4,350 for Year 1. In the ensuing years, we have a budget surplus of $7,150 minus $1,125, or $6,025.

Discovery-Driven Planning

Key objectives

- Understand how discovery-driven planning differs from a standard planning process—and when a discovery-driven approach makes sense
- Identify the four basic steps in discovery-driven planning
- Create an assumptions checklist for each SMART goal
- Prioritize the assumptions
- Design a quick, simple, and inexpensive test for each critical assumption
- Establish a set of checkpoints to decide whether to move forward with your plan, change it, or shelve it

Content summary

De-risking innovation

Your plans are set. Having worked through this workbook, you are ready to implement. But how do you know if your plan will work? Isn't it risky to innovate when children are involved and the odds are uncertain?

The answer can be yes. But *not* innovating in our schools also carries huge risks that are increasingly well known.

Fortunately, we do not have to choose between two risky endeavors. There is a way to de-risk the innovation process: discovery-driven planning.

Discovery-driven planning flips the conventional planning process on its head. In the standard planning process, you make a plan, look at the projected outcomes from the plan, and then, assuming those outcomes look desirable, you implement it.

This approach works well when you have tried something similar before or the innovation is familiar and proven. Specifically, you look to see if three conditions have been met:

1. You have a plan that addresses all of the important details required for success, with a high degree of confidence that the assumptions being made are correct, and those responsible for the implementation understand each important detail.

2. The plan makes as much sense to all members of the organization as they view the world from their own context as it does to the person making the plan, so that everyone will act appropriately and consistently.

3. Outside forces—such as the reaction of the community and students or the impact of other schools, programs, or technology—are reasonably stable and predictable.

If all three of these are true, then go for it! But in most cases, teams implementing a blended-learning program, particularly for the first time, need a very different implementation process.

What is discovery-driven planning?

When launching something that is unfamiliar and unpredictable, with a low ratio of knowledge to hypotheses, educators need to change the planning and design process. The standard planning process won't work because the assumptions, both implicit and explicit, on which the outcomes rest are often wrong.

The key to success will instead often be the ability to test hypotheses and continue to iterate on plans as you gain more information. Therefore, when educators are creating something new that is different from what they have always done previously, they need a different way to create a plan—particularly if the tolerance for failure is low and the need for caution is high, as is so often the case when innovating in education with children.

In a discovery-driven planning process, the key is to start with the desired outcome in mind. From there, the crucial next step is to list all of the assumptions that must prove true to realize the desired outcomes. With the assumptions in hand, the next step is to implement a plan to learn, which means testing, as quickly and cheaply as possible, whether the critical assumptions are reasonable. If the assumptions prove true, then organizations can invest in executing the strategy. If assumptions prove false or uncertain, then organizations can change accordingly or continue to test before they have gone too far. As in the culture module, here we describe a play-by-play set of tactical steps for you to follow to mitigate the risk of failure.

Discovery-driven planning process

Step 1: List desired outcomes.

Step 2: Determine what assumptions must prove true for outcomes to be realized.

Step 3: Implement a plan to learn whether the critical assumptions are reasonable.

Step 4: Implement the strategy when key assumptions prove true.

Check for understanding

The difference between discovery-driven and standard planning

Circle the following statements as true or false.

1. The standard planning process focuses on testing the assumptions underlying the desired outcomes.

   True **False**

2. The standard planning process focuses on whether the projected outcomes appear desirable.

   True **False**

3. A discovery-driven planning process shifts the focus from whether projected outcomes look desirable to testing whether critical assumptions underlying a plan are true.

   True **False**

4. In a discovery-driven planning process, you start with the outcomes that must materialize and then identify the critical assumptions underlying those outcomes and test them to see if you should move forward.

   True **False**

Check for understanding

When to use discovery-driven planning

In the following examples, which planning process would you use: standard or discovery-driven? **Circle** one and briefly explain why.

1. A teacher decides to update a lesson plan that she has used in class for the last ten years with more multimedia examples.

   Standard **Discovery-driven**

   Why?

   ____

   ____

2. A teacher decides to become the first in her entire district to flip her classroom to give students more opportunities to do projects in class.

   Standard **Discovery-driven**

   Why?

   ____

   ____

3. A school decides to scale a blended-learning pilot that has been successful in grades 3 and 4 to grade 5.

   Standard **Discovery-driven**

   Why?

   ____

   ____

4. A school decides to create a school within a school, using a blended, competency-based model, to serve students who had previously dropped out.

   Standard **Discovery-driven**

   Why?

   ____

   ____

Content summary

Start with the outcomes

The first step in a discovery-driven planning process is to identify the outcomes that you want to achieve as a result of the innovation. If everybody knows what the outcomes must look like for the innovation to be worthwhile, then there is no sense in playing a game of Texas Hold 'Em. Just lay the cards out on the table at the outset. What does the final state of the innovation need to do? What are you trying to accomplish? And how will you know you have been successful?

The good news is that in creating your SMART goals, you have already defined success and completed this step.

Create an assumptions checklist

The second step is where the real work begins. With the desired goals and outcomes identified, compile an assumptions checklist. Referring to the plan you have built over the previous modules, list all of the assumptions being made that must prove true in order for the desired outcomes to materialize.

Be exhaustive. All of the assumptions that schools make implicitly should be on the table, including the use of time and school schedules, space, and staffing. In Figure 2.1, we offer some ideas to help you brainstorm. One way to capture the full range of these assumptions is to go section by section through this book and lay out all of the design elements being put in place, including the type of team implementing the innovation and who is on the team; the student experience; the teacher experience; the software, hardware, infrastructure, and facilities; the blended-learning model and where it is being implemented (whether in a core academic area or an area of nonconsumption); the culture; the implementation plan; and the budget.

Figure 2.1: Be Expansive about the Assumptions

TEAM	STUDENT EXPERIENCE	TEACHER EXPERIENCE	SOFTWARE	HARDWARE
• Are the right people at the table? • Does the team leader have the right level of authority? • Do we have enough senior leader support?	• Do some of our students need different experiences to be successful? • Are there enough opportunities for them to have fun with friends in the course of working?	• Are we asking teachers to do things for which they are not trained? • Are teachers matched to the right roles where they can feel success?	• Does the software have enough instructional minutes? • Is the content rigorous enough? • Will it provide actionable, easily understood data?	• Is the hardware durable enough? • Do we have enough Wi-Fi? • Can we afford upgrades? • Do we have enough backup equipment if things break?

FACILITY	LEARNING MODEL	CULTURE	BUDGET	IMPLEMENTATION
• Do we have enough electrical outlets? • Does the furniture match the experiences for students? • Does the space reinforce the desired culture?	• Are we asking students to stay in rotations for too long? • Does this model provide opportunities that match the experiences we want to offer students?	• Will the process for switching between modalities work for students? • Is implementing blended learning a priority for the team members? • Do we have the right norms in place for students?	• Have we accounted for device replacement costs and insurance? • Are our savings assumptions realistic?	• Have we sequenced the tasks correctly? • Have we given ourselves enough time for community outreach?

For example, one way to work through the assumptions embedded in the budget is to examine every line item listed in the preceding module and pressure-test each. If you said you would buy fifteen software licenses at $10 per student, for example, key assumptions would be the price point and the number of software licenses.

By cataloging all of these assumptions—and their implicit underlying components—you will assemble a comprehensive list of assumptions. That means everything from "This math software will be rigorous enough" to "Our teachers will have the data they need to intervene in the right ways" to "The time we give students to learn is enough for them to master the curriculum."

This process of listing out assumptions should take a day or two, and it is time spent well. Sometimes the list of assumptions at this stage will number more than one hundred! We also recommend having people at the table in this brainstorming exercise who represent a variety of departments and perspectives, so that the assumptions list will be exhaustive and will help the leader understand where people within an organization do and do not agree.

To assist you in the brainstorming process and to give you a sense of the range of assumptions that you may be making—either implicitly or explicitly—in your plan, we offer a list of twenty-five assumptions that other school teams have identified.

Assumptions

1. Master schedule includes special ed. teacher.
2. Teachers buy in (want to do this) and want to work together to teach all kids together.
3. Teachers have capacity to do this type of work.
4. I will convince the district to fully fund my project, meaning:
   a. Computers;
   b. Math software;
   c. Aide;
   d. PD time will work within 64 min. after school site–based collaboration time.
5. Collaborative learning environment will lead to sustainability (point person, training, cross training).
6. The 70 min. block will work: tier 1 instruction, intervention, and acceleration.
7. My team and I can make this happen by the start of the next school year.
8. Computer schedule will work for fifth graders and for their pod-mates.
9. Math software will work on BYOD.
10. Math software will work on the district's old computers.
11. Existing technology will last the school year.
12. We have enough headphones to last the year.

13. We have enough students willing to bring their own headphones.
14. We have enough mice to last the year.
15. We have enough students able to bring their own devices.
16. Substitutes will understand the plan.
17. Substitutes will be able to execute the plan.
18. We will be able to train teachers to read and use reports by the start of year.
19. Kids will be fairly independent on the new program from the start (with minimal aide support).
20. The technology will work daily (lead to a backup plan).
21. A staff member is available and has capacity to handle student provisioning.
22. Parents will be comfortable with their children doing middle school work in elementary school concurrently.
23. The math software is suitable as my only intervention tool.
24. The number of fifth graders we are serving will stay the same.
25. There is sufficient monitoring to help with transition to other fifth-grade rooms.

Draft your plan

Assumptions brainstorm

Now it's your turn. Fill out your assumptions in the first column in the Discovery-Driven Planning Table. If you're not sure whether something is an assumption or if you have any questions about it, then write it down. At this stage, more is better. (Ignore the other columns for now; we will return to them later in this module.)

For your other SMART goals, we have provided space in the back of the book for you to do the exercises in this module.

Discovery-Driven Planning Table

Assumption	Risk (1, 2, 3)	Confidence (1, 2, 3)	Rank (Avg.)	Test

Content summary

Rank your assumptions

Once you are done compiling all of the assumptions, the next job is to rank the assumptions from the most to the least crucial. We have found that having the same group of individuals ask two questions about each assumption is the best way to accomplish this.

First, ask what could happen if you are wrong about an assumption. In other words, which of these assumptions, if proved untrue, would most seriously derail the success of the project? If the assumption is wrong, will it be catastrophic to the project? Will it require a major overhaul of the plan? Is the impact just minor, and does it require only a few tweaks? Or is being wrong no big deal, as it will have no impact on the plan? If being wrong will be catastrophic to the project, assign it a priority value of 1; if it's no big deal, assign it a 3. A rank of 2 is in between. Fill in the Risk column in the Discovery-Driven Planning Table with your scores.

Second, ask how confident you are that each assumption is correct. A fun test of how confident people are is to see if they are willing to give up one year's salary if they are wrong—meaning they have a high degree of confidence that they know the answer. Perhaps they are willing to give up only one week's salary if they are wrong? Or one day's worth? Or maybe they aren't willing to bet any of their salary because they have no sense of whether the assumption is correct. Assign a value based on confidence. A rank of 1 signals no confidence that the assumption is correct, whereas a rank of 3 suggests high confidence that it is correct. Enter these numbers in the Confidence column of the Discovery-Driven Planning Table.

After rating all of the assumptions, average the scores and enter the averages in the Rank column of the Discovery-Driven Planning Table. This gives you your ordered assumption checklist.

Those assumptions with a rank close to 1.0—because they are the most crucial to the project's success and yet you have the least confidence in whether they are right—are the most important assumptions to pay attention to in the next step. Those closer to a 3.0 are not as critical for the project's success, and you can therefore afford to test them later.

To illustrate, the assumption about the cost of the software from earlier (being able to buy fifteen software licenses at $10 per student) would probably be closer to a 3.0 than a 1.0. Why? If you're wrong about the cost of the software—it's more than $10 per student—it is probably not much more than that, so it is unlikely to change your plan much. And when it comes to the confidence rating, you are likely to have some certainty around the cost figure, or at least know the ballpark range.

Bucket the assumptions in three zones. Zone 1 will be those with scores ranging from 1.0 to 1.6; these assumptions are the most critical and urgent to test. Zone 2 will be those with scores ranging from 1.7 to 2.3. Zone 3, those with scores ranging from 2.4 to 3.0, are the least urgent to test.

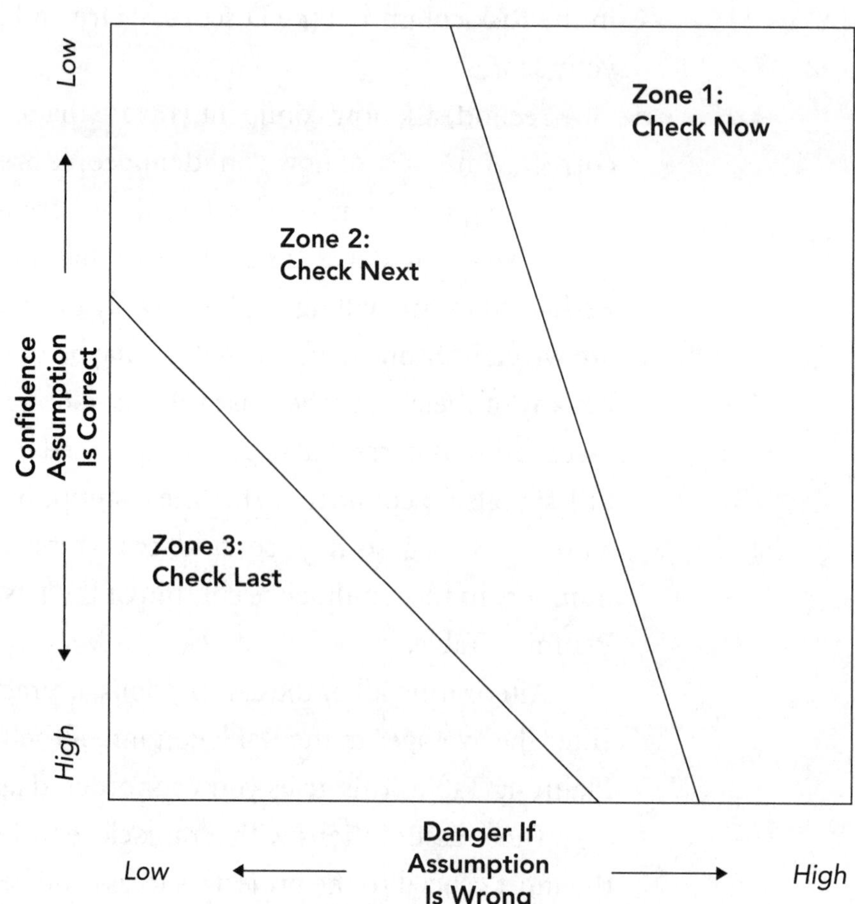

Map them on the graph here so you can clearly see where your assumptions lie, as well as which are the most important to check, and why. Doing this will also allow you to think about how the assumptions compare to one another within the zones.

Implement a plan—to learn more

With the prioritized assumptions checklist in hand, the next step is to implement a plan to test the validity of the assumptions. Plan to check the most important assumptions—those in Zone 1—first because those are the assumptions with the least confidence behind them that are also the most crucial to the project's success.

In the initial stages of planning, the tests should be as simple, inexpensive, and quick as possible. They should simply provide a sense—not a clear answer—about whether the most critical assumptions are reasonable. For example, it is a good idea to look at other schools—like the ones written about in *Blended*—to see whether the assumptions hold water before going too far down a road. Reading the existing research, having early conversations, or creating quick mock-ups or prototypes makes sense. A prototype is anything that helps communicate the idea of what you are doing, which can mean everything from mock-ups and models to simulations and role-playing experiences. It is often helpful to create what people call the "minimum viable product"; this means slapping together the simplest product or prototype that allows the testing of the salient assumptions as quickly as possible. More concretely, perhaps a key assumption being made concerns the rigor of a math program. A school could, as an initial test, read about the program and talk to others who use it; for a second test, the school could then ask for one license for the math program so that its teachers can poke around and see if it passes their own smell test for being rigorous enough. If it passes, the school might then implement a third test by finding a place—such as in summer school or after school—to pilot the math program for a couple of weeks before buying it and using it for all of its students for an entire year. And it might do this for a couple of other programs as well.

The following are some ways to creatively and quickly test your assumptions.

Test creatively: Keep it simple, keep it cheap

- Quickly create a "good enough" prototype.
- Talk to students and parents.
- Talk to internal resources.
- Talk to other schools doing something similar.
- Visit other schools.
- Look to your history.
- Read the research.
- Identify early milestones.
- Talk to the business manager to make sure it is sustainable.
- Talk to experts in the field.
- Conduct a focus group.
- Launch a pilot, perhaps in the summer or after school.

Sample tests

To help you with the tests, we have included a series of them that address a variety of assumptions. After you read through these, go back to the Discovery-Driven Planning Table to write down the tests that you will use to test your ideas initially.

Assumption: Our Station Rotation structure for second-grade students creates enough flexibility for teachers to truly personalize for each student—as in, students won't get locked into groupings inappropriate for their learning needs—such that we will see student achievement soar.

> **Early test:** Talk to other schools that have implemented Station Rotation to see how they have balanced the need for structure with the need for flexibility and how they have evolved, as well as what student achievement has been.

Assumption: Stakeholders—students, parents, teachers, administrators, and community leaders—will support the transition to and implementation of our blended-learning initiative.

Early tests:

- Talk with students about their current and hoped-for school experiences.
- Invite early-adopter teachers to lead reflective teachers' meetings.
- Invite active parent and community participation at initial and future board meetings where everyone is welcome to voice any concern throughout the pilot.

Assumption: Our blended-learning initiative will fulfill our students' "job to be done" of productive fun with friends at school.

Early test: Visit other schools that have implemented similar blended-learning initiatives to observe students there and collect data.

Assumption: Our administrators will take on the challenge of leading transformative change and supporting teachers at all times.

Early tests:

- Counsel with administrators about their perceptions of blended learning and the cultures of change and support in their schools.
- Look to past examples in your school's history of major change to learn how administrators handled those instances.

Assumption: Our campus Wi-Fi network will support a large number of devices used at once throughout the campus.

Early tests:

- Ask IT administrators at other blended-learning schools.
- Run a summer practice test with teachers' usage in place of students'.

Decide on next steps

The last step is to decide whether to continue implementing the strategy.

You should set a checkpoint—a specific date when the tests of several of the assumptions should be completed—so that the team can come together and evaluate what it has learned. The period leading up to the first checkpoint could last one month and be designed to give team members time to study other blended-learning schools and test some (but not all) of the assumptions at a high level.

If your assumptions are proving true, then keep moving forward to the next checkpoint.

If they are not—as will more than likely be the case—you have a few options. Perhaps you can tweak the plan to keep moving forward; for example, maybe the math software an educator had planned to use will be good for only twenty minutes of instruction a day rather than thirty minutes; this means the rotation schedule will have to be adjusted.

Alternatively, there may need to be bigger adjustments. Perhaps you need a different team to implement the blended-learning model you have designed in an area of nonconsumption where there will be more time to fine-tune the innovation before it must be scaled to the entire school.

Or finally, perhaps the assumptions underlying the success of the plan are wildly unrealistic, and the plan just won't work. If this is the case, then there is an opportunity to shelve the plan before too much money has been invested and the stakes have become too high to abandon the idea.

If you do decide to move forward, don't just move to implement the plan whole hog.

Look at your assumptions again and brainstorm tests that are more comprehensive, precise, and perhaps more costly than the previous ones. The key is to keep your tests as low-cost and quick as possible, but precise enough that you will gain more knowledge than you had before. Assumptions that you didn't test before might now be tested. The important thing is not to invest a lot of time and resources early before knowing whether the assumptions are proving true—or at least are in the right ballpark.

Establish a rhythm for your tests. Set up more checkpoints—perhaps the second one will occur in another month and a third will be a month after that. The tests during the second checkpoint might include an analysis of the software market. Further down the line, a checkpoint might include a working prototype or pilot of the blended-learning model, and then the launch of the blended-learning model itself. You will have the opportunity to map out your own checkpoints in the next module as you develop your implementation plan.

At each checkpoint, the team will gain new information. An assumption that seemed correct at a previous checkpoint may be revealed to be more complex than it was originally thought to be. That's OK. And if the team learns that ultimately the assumptions are unrealistic and that it won't be able to pull off the program, that is not a reason for despair. Fast failure is a success; the team learned that the idea would not work before wasting a lot of time and money implementing a plan that wouldn't work. The key is to celebrate each time a decision is made. People should not feel that they have to defend a pet idea; the victory is in learning more about an assumption, not in proving that someone is right or wrong.

Ultimately, as the team makes adjustments and iterates, it may find that it is going down a path with assumptions that are proving true. Even though the design and plan that is emerging and gradually being implemented is different from the one that was foreseen originally, if it will be successful in realizing the desired outcomes, then that's a resounding success—and the ultimate value of the discovery-driven process.

View rubric and assess your plan

Refining your discovery-driven plan

With your Discovery-Driven Planning Table complete, you are now ready to develop the last section of your blended-learning plan: the implementation schedule. The tests that you identified in this module to check assumptions will be essential activities to add to your implementation plan as key checkpoints.

Before beginning that final planning project, check your work in this module. Use the Discovery-Driven Planning Rubric that follows to verify that your discovery-driven plan, as contained in the Discovery-Driven Planning Table, is exceptional.

Discovery-Driven Planning Rubric

	Exceptional 3	Advanced 2	Basic 1	Inadequate 0
Assumptions list	Provides an **exhaustive** list of assumptions that **reflects all parts of the plan**.	Provides a list of assumptions that **reflects most parts of the plan**.	Provides a **partial** list that evidences a basic analysis of the plan.	List is mostly **incomplete.**
Prioritization of assumptions	Prioritizes the assumptions **accurately** by evaluating the level of danger if the assumption proves wrong and the level of confidence that the assumption is true.	Prioritizes assumptions **mostly** correctly, although some choices are questionable.	Makes an effort to prioritize, but prioritization does not consider the level of danger if the assumption proves wrong and the level of confidence that the assumption is true.	Assumptions are **not prioritized**.
Plan to test and learn	Proposes a **simple, inexpensive plan** to test and learn to ensure that key assumptions prove true.	Proposes a plan to test and learn, **but a few aspects may be overly complicated or expensive**.	Proposes a plan to test and learn, but **many aspects are overly complicated and/or expensive**.	Proposes a plan, but it **does not focus on key assumptions OR** is incomplete.

APPENDIX

Check for understanding: The difference between discovery-driven and standard planning

1. False
2. True
3. True
4. True

Check for understanding: When to use discovery-driven planning

1. Standard. This isn't fundamentally changing the lesson, just improving it, such that the teacher probably has a good upfront sense of how the addition of multimedia will impact the class.
2. Discovery driven. Although many have implemented the Flipped Classroom, this teacher has not, nor has anyone close to her. Unpredictable behaviors and actions are bound to occur. The teacher's ratio of knowledge to assumptions is low.
3. Standard. The pilot has already been successful, so there is a fair amount of knowledge about how it works. Now it's about scaling, which is likely to come down to getting the operational details correct more than unearthing surprises before they occur.
4. Discovery driven. The school is creating a radically new model with little knowledge of how it will work. Following a discovery-driven process to mitigate the risks will be key.

Implementation Plan

Key objectives

- ○ Identify the components of your operation that must change in order for you to implement your design, and specify how they must change.
- ○ Develop milestones, checkpoints, and a timeline for when and how you will implement each task that the pilot and rollout phases require.

Content summary

From design to practice

Earlier in this workbook, you had the opportunity to design a new vision for the student and teacher experiences, with jobs-to-be-done theory as a lens to give your efforts predictability and focus.

You began by understanding the jobs that students have in their lives; this is the first level in the architecture of a job. For the second level, you brainstormed all the experiences that you have to provide to get the jobs done perfectly. This type of design thinking not only redounds to the happiness and motivation that students feel for your program but also helps you earn student buy-in for working hard toward achieving the results that you want them to achieve as part of *your* job.

Once you understand all those experiences, you can implement the third level: integrate your operations by knitting together the right assets that are required to provide each of the experiences necessary to do the job perfectly. This level requires understanding the resources you need and how to implement them in a way that will deliver the experiences you've planned.

In this module of the workbook, you have the opportunity to think through that integration process step-by-step and develop a practical plan for turning theory and design into reality at your schools of implementation.

Apply the learning

What to integrate and how

Refer to your first SMART goal and the new student and teacher experiences you designed to achieve the goal. What components of your operations must change in order for you to implement this new design, and how must they change? Revisit each previous module of this workbook, one by one, and list the components in the Integration Table here. An example is provided. Be sure to consider any regulatory waivers and policy changes as well.

Integration Table

Component	What must change?	How must it change?
Student experience (Schedules, curriculum, mentoring, tutoring, apprenticeships, wellness, access to data, etc.)	*Example:* Schedule for P.E.	*Example:* Increase length of P.E. blocks to increase physical exercise time

Component	What must change?	How must it change?
Teacher and staff roles and responsibilities (including resource specialists and instructional assistants)		
Teacher and staff recruitment and training		
Teacher motivators		
Virtual environment: software, LMS, middleware, and hardware		

Component	What must change?	How must it change?
Physical environment: facilities, Wi-Fi, electrical outlets, furniture		
Culture		
Budget: revenue and funding, cost reductions		
Communication and stakeholder buy-in		

Component	What must change?	How must it change?
Discovery-driven planning processes		

Draft your plan

Top 5 project management software programs for students

These programs could work well for educators, too, because they rank high for affordability, ease of use, and strength of collaboration tools.

Teamwork: *www.teamwork.com*

Glasscubes: *www.glasscubes.com*

Redbooth: *www.redbooth.com*

Basecamp: *www.basecamp.com*

5pm: *www.5pmweb.com*

Source: Reviews.com, "The 5 Best Project Management Software for Students," *http://www.reviews.com/project-management-software/students/*.

Milestone mapping

Now that you've identified what must change and how it must change, you can turn this set of tasks into concrete milestones. A milestone is an action or event that marks significant progress in the implementation of your program.

Go through each line of the Integration Table and convert the item into a milestone. on a new chart, such as the Gantt Chart Template that follows. For example, if the line item on the Integration Table refers to the task of increasing physical fitness time, your milestone on the new chart could be "Expanded P.E. schedule is in place for all middle school students at Alpha campus." Develop a timeline that shows your key milestones over the next three years. Keep these guidelines in mind:

- A Gantt is a chart with horizontal lines that show the time period when each work stream will be under way, with a star to mark the milestone at the end of the work stream. You can complete the following Gantt Chart Template here, or feel free to use any project management software or other format that you prefer. For example, Education Elements offers a technology tool called Touchpoint that helps districts manage their various initiatives (see *https://www.edelements.com/education-project-management-tool-touchpoint*).
- The milestones should include discovery-driven planning checkpoints (which you learned about in the preceding module), such as to analyze the software market to test whether the content you need exists, and then one month later to conduct a focus group about your devices to test the assumption that they are adequate. Establish a monthly cadence of checkpoints.
- The timeline should show both a pilot phase and a rollout phase, with extra detail and planning evidenced for the pilot phase.

Gantt Chart Template

ID	Task	No. of quarters to complete	Year 1				Year 2				Year 3			
			Q1	Q2	Q3	Q4	Q1	Q2	Q3	Q4	Q1	Q2	Q3	Q4
Example	Expand P.E. schedule	2		→	→	*Milestone: Expanded P.E. schedules in place for all middle school students at Alpha campus.								
1														
2														
3														
4														
5														

6														
7														
8														
9														
10														
11														
12														

View rubric and assess your plan

Refining your implementation plan

Use the following Implementation Rubric to help you evaluate your Integration Table and Gantt Chart Template. It describes the criteria that distinguish an exceptional vision for implementation (3) from one that is advanced (2), basic (1), or inadequate (0).

Implementation Rubric

	Exceptional 3	Advanced 2	Basic 1	Inadequate 0
What must change?	Considers **all parts of the blended-learning plan** to develop a thorough understanding of the components of the operation that must change to deliver the new learning design.	Considers **most parts of the plan** to develop an understanding of the components of the operation that must change to deliver the new learning design.	Considers **only part of the plan**; the team does not have an understanding of the components of the operation that must change.	**Does not consider the plan** when deciding what must change in the current operation.
Milestones	Proposes a list of milestones for each year that meets all requirements. *Requirements:* • The list is comprehensive and organized. • The milestones are specific, reasonable, and sufficient to achieve the desired outcomes. • Milestones include discovery-driven planning checkpoints. • Includes both pilot and rollout phases, with extra detail provided for the pilot phase.	The list of milestones meets most requirements.	The list of milestones meets one or two requirements.	**Ignores** the work of identifying key milestones.

	Exceptional 3	Advanced 2	Basic 1	Inadequate 0
Pilot tests	The milestones include a **realistic** pilot test and a **sound** plan for implementing the necessary changes to establish the pilot.	Proposes a **mostly** realistic and sound pilot test plan.	Proposes a **partial** pilot test plan.	**Overlooks** the pilot-testing phase.

Continue to revise your implementation plan until you earn full points according to the rubric.

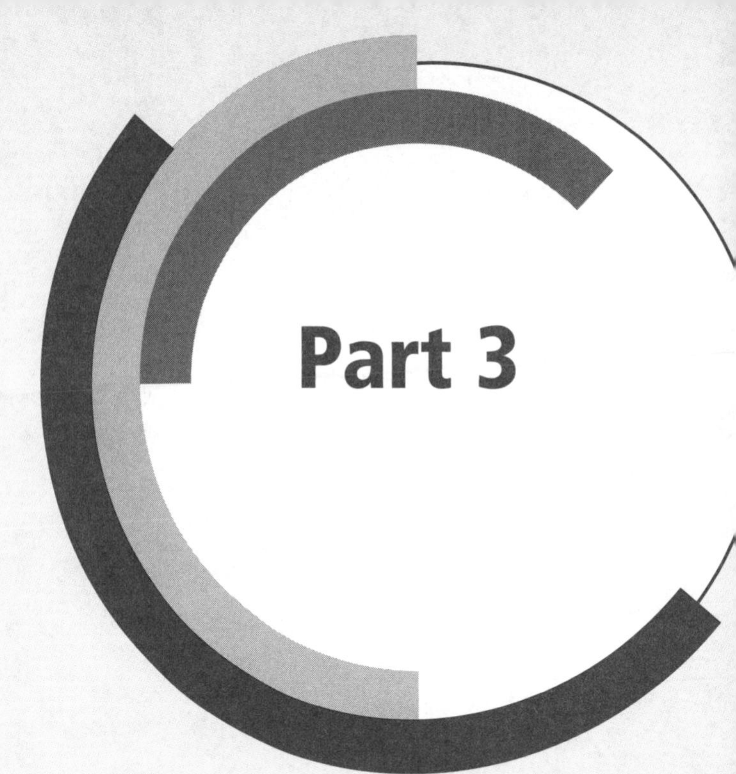

Polishing Your Plan

Finishing Touches and Next Steps

Key objectives

- ○ Name your blended-learning initiative
- ○ Create the final drafts of your blended-learning plans
- ○ Seek feedback, iterate, and blend

Content summary

Naming your blended-learning initiative

Congratulations! You have designed your blended-learning initiative—or initiatives. You have a strong sense of what they are about—the problems you are solving or goals you are trying to achieve; what constitutes success; the educational visions and plans to deliver the results for students; and how you're going to put the designs into action.

The penultimate step in the process is to name each of your plans and create cover pages for them with, for example, your district, school, or classroom name and contact information for the primary project manager whom you selected in the team selection work in Module 2.2.

Sounds simple, right? Don't overlook it. Naming your plan will help make it even more "real" and help you commit to executing it. It will give you a shorthand way to refer to what you are doing and help you build a communications strategy around your effort so that key stakeholders throughout your school community understand what you are doing, why you are doing it, and how it will benefit them.

Other groups have created resources to help teams create critical communications plans. (See, for example, Education Elements and The Learning Accelerator's *Communications Planning for Innovation in Education* [www.edelements.com/personalized-learning-communications-guide].) The focus here is on naming your project.

The reason the step occurs here, rather than at the beginning, is that it is hard to name something before it's fully designed. If you name an initiative too early, before it's baked, that name can become a trap and keep you locked into a certain vision for a project at the expense of a robust design process that could help you create a very novel idea that does not fit into any preconceived boxes. But now that you have done all the design work, you are ready to commit to a name.

Choosing the right name is important. The name is a critical element of the brand, a term that means the unique words and symbols that identify the project. In many cases, a brand suggests (either subtly or directly) the benefit that the solution provides. A brand serves as a workhorse for the project as it sends a message to the outside world about the project's value.

Many schools say that one of the toughest parts of implementing blended learning is the communication piece. Leaders must convey the reasons for the changes to their parents, teachers, school board, and other stakeholders. The up-front work of developing a name and brand for the project is an important initial step toward broadcasting a positive message.

Schools use different frames of reference for choosing a brand. A few of the most common naming conventions include metaphor-based names, descriptive names, or acronyms.

Baltimore County Public Schools (BCPS), a large district in Maryland, has used names to its advantage multiple times. For example, it appointed a student committee to develop the brand name for its blended-learning initiative. The students decided to use an acronym and named the project S.T.A.T., short for "Students and Teachers Accessing Tomorrow." The choice was clever because "STAT" is also a medical term for "urgent"—which helped convey the importance of the initiative that has helped transform the district's schools.

Another time, BCPS used a descriptive naming convention to rebrand its Alternative Education Office. The name had a negative connotation as being an undesirable place for students, despite its being a place of important innovation within the district. BCPS rebranded it as the Office of Educational Options, which offered a more positive spin as a place creating and offering critical options for students, one where they could discover their passions and learn.

Here are some examples of powerful names in each of the three categories:

- Metaphor: Rocketship Public Schools, Summit Public Schools, Springboard Education

- Descriptive: Operation Graduation, Personalized Literacy Program, Hands-On Science
- Acronym: S.T.A.T., ACCESS (Alabama Connecting Classrooms, Educators, and Students Statewide)

Brainstorm the options

What's your name?

Brainstorm several brand names for your projects in each of the three categories in the Name Brainstorm chart here.

One question that could help your brainstorming is this: "In what circumstances will this program help our students and schools?" Then choose a name that conveys that opportunity. For example, one district we have worked with developed a plan to accelerate more students from the proficient to the advanced level of academic performance. Accordingly, the district named its program *Elevate*.

Name Brainstorm

Metaphor Ideas	Descriptive Ideas	Acronym Ideas

Review the list. Strike out any ideas that make any of the following common branding errors:

- Difficult to spell or pronounce
- Nonstandard spelling
- Use of jargon that only educators would understand
- Too long

- Too cute; not professional
- Overused or clichéd

Now look through the list and consider a few other ideas. How many words do you want your name to be? Many educators like to choose succinct names with no more than two words that pack a punch; others like something that is longer and more descriptive. To further narrow your list, think through your preferences by brainstorming others' programs that have resonated with you.

Finally, think through how symbolic you want your name to be versus how concrete. There is no right answer here per se—our only strong advice is to avoid made-up words in an effort to be overly cute.

From the remaining ideas, decide on the best name to brand your initiative. Use the space here to jot down any logo or symbols that you may want to use as well.

Final name, logo, and symbol ideas

Bringing It All Together

Create your final draft

This last section is where we bring everything together. Included here are the complete blended-learning rubric and the blended-learning template. Pieces of both have appeared throughout the other modules, but here is where we put it all together—and you have the opportunity to create your final draft.

As you have worked through the book, you may have learned that you need more or different people involved on your team to get your design right or to correctly implement it. This is a great time to write down your final team, have your final team edit all of the answers you have recorded in the workbook up until now, and together develop a final draft.

Rubric for blended-learning plan

Problem Statement Rubric

Exceptional 3	Advanced 2	Basic 1	Inadequate 0
Identifies at least one core problem and/or one nonconsumption problem. *Requirements:* • Either goes deep by solving one root problem or goes wide by undertaking more than one project to address instructional gaps and/or environmental barriers. • Problem is based on barriers to achievement. • Uses quantitative data to show that the problem is significant. • Problem does not focus on "technology for technology's sake"; rather, technology is subordinate to a student-centered mission.	Identifies at least one problem, but is **less than convincing** with one or more of the requirements (e.g., includes quantitative data, but data is not used to illustrate the significance of the problem).	Identifies at least one problem, but **clearly fails to satisfy one to two of the requirements** (e.g., does not include quantitative data).	The answer **does not identify a clear academic problem**, or the statement does not meet **any** of the requirements.

SMART Goals Rubric

Exceptional 3	Advanced 2	Basic 1	Inadequate 0
States a goal that is specific, measurable, assignable, realistic, and time-related (SMART). *Requirements:* • Uses numbers to quantify the improvement that the team plans to achieve. • Identifies specific metrics for Year 1, Year 2, and Year 3, with more narrow, formative, groundwork-laying metrics in the early years and broader, longer-lead-time metrics in the later years. • Sequences these targets in a realistic way, so as not to assume that broad gains in student achievement will happen in Year 1. • Can be assigned to the right leader when the time comes.	States a SMART goal, but **does not meet one requirement.**	States a SMART goal, but **does not meet two to three requirements.**	Does not state a goal **OR** states a goal that does not meet the requirements.

Team Selection Rubric

Exceptional 3	Advanced 2	Basic 1	Inadequate 0
Matches the **optimal type of team** to the scope of each task for each SMART goal and explains why this is a viable match.	Proposes a type of team that will work for the scope of each task for each SMART goal, but, based on the theory of what team is best for what type of problem, **a better option is available.**	Makes an effort to identify a team, but overall **misapplies the theory**.	Does not select a team or **does not use the theory** to explain why the choice was made.

Team Member Selection Rubric

	Exceptional 3	Advanced 2	Basic 1	Inadequate 0
Team member selection	Thoughtful selection of members with **good reasons for each one**, based on the following requirements. *Requirements:* • Range of roles and individual selection matches the range of experiences needed to execute on SMART goal. • Team brings valuable skills, proper authority, and relevant experience. • Takes into account stakeholders who have the authority to block an initiative. • The number of individuals on the team matches the range of roles; there are not too many or too few people on the team. • Integrates community members beyond employees (e.g., parents, students, etc.), as appropriate.	Rationale for selection of members **meets most requirements**.	Rationale for selection of members **meets few requirements**.	There is **no rationale for selection of members OR** composition does not correspond to a specific type of team.

	Exceptional 3	Advanced 2	Basic 1	Inadequate 0
Project manager	Identifies a **qualified** manager who will oversee implementation; **describes the previous track record and time that the leader can devote to the project.**	Identifies a qualified manager, but **description leaves some questions** about the manager's track record and/or time the manager can devote to the project.	Identifies a qualified manager, but the **description is very incomplete or misguided.**	Does not identify a clear manager of the team, **OR** the description does not give any evidence of the manager being able to handle the role.

Student Experience Rubric

	Exceptional 3	Advanced 2	Basic 1	Inadequate 0
Design work	Designs a plan that **shows students' daily and weekly experiences** for each project from at least two perspectives; the plan includes **varied academic and social experiences**.	Provides a complete design, but it leaves **some question** about what the student experience will involve.	Provides a basic design, but it leaves **major questions** about what the student experience will involve.	Does not provide a tangible design beyond buzzwords.
Application of jobs-to-be-done theory	Designs a **comprehensive plan** that unlocks students' intrinsic motivations of feeling successful each day and having fun with friends while accounting for other barriers that require remediation (e.g., physical activity, work-related commitments).	Designs a plan that unlocks students' intrinsic motivations but **does not account for other barriers**.	Designs a plan, but it **does not unlock students' intrinsic motivations**.	Does not present any compelling set of experiences.

	Exceptional 3	Advanced 2	Basic 1	Inadequate 0
Link	Provides a **fully reasonable rationale** for why the new student experience will mitigate the problem identified in Section 1: Rallying Cry.	Presents a **mostly** reasonable link between the design and the problem.	Presents a **somewhat** reasonable link between the design and the problem.	Does not connect the design to the problem.
Competency-based learning	Incorporates the principles of competency-based learning to ensure that students will have the opportunity to work on higher-order skills and will not move in lockstep pace with the class at all times.	Incorporates the principles of competency-based learning, **but some parts are unrealistic or too vague**.	Attempts to incorporate competency-based learning, but **many parts are unrealistic or too vague**.	Does not incorporate the principles of competency-based learning, **OR** requires all students to move in lockstep.
Mentorship and coaching	Incorporates the principles of sound, one-on-one mentorship and coaching such that students will have the support and relationships they need to succeed in their particular circumstances.	Incorporates the principles of sound, one-on-one mentorship and coaching, but **some parts are unrealistic or too vague**.	Attempts to incorporate the principles of sound, one-on-one mentorship and coaching, but **many parts are unrealistic or too vague**.	Does not incorporate the principles of sound, one-on-one mentorship and coaching.

Amplifying Motivators Rubric

	Exceptional 3	Advanced 2	Basic 1	Inadequate 0
Job motivators	Describes at least **two powerful motivators** that the design seeks to deliver to improve teachers' job satisfaction. Does not confuse a motivator with a hygiene factor.	Describes at least **one powerful motivator** that the design seeks to deliver to improve teachers' job satisfaction. Does not confuse a motivator with a hygiene factor.	Makes an effort to describe at least one motivator, but the design is **ordinary** from the teacher motivation perspective and does not allow for professional advancement.	Does not name any motivators.
Implementation strategy	Describes a concrete, realistic strategy for amplifying these motivators.	Describes strategy for amplifying these motivators, but **small parts might be vague or unrealistic**.	Describes a strategy for amplifying these motivators, but **large parts are vague or unrealistic**.	**Does not describe a strategy** for amplifying the motivator(s) named.

Physical and Virtual Environment Rubric

	Exceptional 3	Advanced 2	Basic 1	Inadequate 0
Audit	Provides a **full summary** of a formal audit report that examines the quantity and useful life of hardware and software assets, the quality of Wi-Fi, and the availability of suitable facilities for the blended program(s).	Provides a summary of a formal audit report, but it is **missing some key summative information**.	Provides some data about the existing environment, but it has **big data gaps**.	Audit report is **missing** or mostly incomplete.

	Exceptional 3	Advanced 2	Basic 1	Inadequate 0
Analysis of audit	Evidences an **accurate and thorough** understanding of the ways that the existing environment already accommodates the proposed blended-learning design and the ways in which it will need to change.	Evidences an adequate understanding of these issues, but one part of the analysis is **not thorough** and/or has **inaccuracies**.	Evidences some thought about these issues, but the analysis is largely **superficial** and/or **inaccurate**.	Analysis is **missing OR** does not relate to the audit.
Vision for improvement	Presents a new vision for the physical and virtual environment that **aligns neatly** with and **supports** the new learning design.	Presents a new vision for the environment that is aligned to the learning design, but **one part of the learning design might not be supported.**	Presents a vision for the environment that is **largely incomplete**.	Vision for improvement is **missing** or does not support the new learning design.

Choose the Model Rubric

	Exceptional 3	Advanced 2	Basic 1	Inadequate 0
Model selection	Names and justifies the **appropriate models** of blended learning as the engines to power the design, given the site's circumstances.	Names the model(s) that will be used and explains why, but the fit is **less than optimal**, given the site's circumstances.	Names the model(s) that will be used, but the fit is **questionable**, given the site's circumstances.	Names the model(s), but the choice is **unreasonable**.

Culture Rubric

	Exceptional 3	Advanced 2	Basic 1	Inadequate 0
List of problems or tasks	Provides a list of **3–4 high-priority problems or tasks** that will recur or are likely to arise in a student-centered blended-learning environment.	Provides a list, although the problems or tasks are **not the highest priority** in this kind of environment.	Provides **only 1–2 high-priority problems or tasks;** other problems/tasks are low priority.	Evidences a **lack of understanding** about what a recurring problem or task is in this kind of environment.
Proposed routines	Proposes routines aligned to the problem/task that are **all** of the following: efficient, student driven, and sustainable over time.	Proposes routines aligned to the problem/task that are **most** of the following: efficient, student driven, and sustainable over time.	Proposes routines, but they **do meet the criteria** to be successful.	Routines are **not aligned** to the problem/task.
Promotion	Proposes a plan for promoting the new processes until they become **planted deeply into the culture** across the system.	Proposes a plan for promoting the new processes, but it is **less than comprehensive.**	Describes how the team will promote the process, but it is **superficial or unlikely to work.**	**Skips** the important step of promoting the culture.

Budget Narrative Rubric

	Exceptional 3	Advanced 2	Basic 1	Inadequate 0
Sources/ Uses of funds	Provides a **complete** narrative of key one-time and recurring sources and uses of funds required over a five-year time frame. These sources of funds may include "internally generated" resource reallocation or partnership opportunities.	Provides a mostly comprehensive narrative of sources and uses of funds, but may be **missing a few key costs/ revenues**.	Provides a partial narrative of sources and uses of funds, but **does not include many of the likely one-time and recurring costs/ revenues**.	Provides **no specifics** as to use of funds or revenue sources to fund the initiative.

	Exceptional 3	Advanced 2	Basic 1	Inadequate 0
Sustaina-bility	Articulates a plan for how the district or school intends to **sustain operational changes** necessary after incremental, one-time funding has been exhausted.	Discusses sustainability, but the plan **may lead to minor budget deficits later in implementation**.	Discusses sustainability, but the plan **will likely lead to minor budget deficits**.	Does **not address sustainability OR** assumes that grant funding will continue to make the initiative work on an ongoing basis.
Creativity	Identifies opportunities to fund and scale **creatively** through cost-saving efforts, partnerships, in-kind services, or other solutions to help scale successfully with limited incremental funding in the long term.	Identifies opportunities to fund and scale that show a modest effort to think creatively, but **one to two ideas may be unrealistic or overlooked**.	Presents an idea or two to fund and scale creatively, but **does not evidence the kind of creativity that will lead to an actual ability to pull off the plan** with limited incremental funding in the long term.	Presents **no creative sources of revenue or savings**.
Table	Supports narrative with a simple spreadsheet or table that includes costs and revenue for a five-year planning period. The numbers match the narrative.	Provides a spreadsheet or table of costs and revenue for a five-year planning period that is **mostly aligned to the narrative**.	Provides a spreadsheet or table, but the **numbers in it are not aligned to the narrative** and/or there are **major gaps** or inaccuracies.	Table is **incomplete OR** does not create a balanced budget or one with a surplus.

Discovery-Driven Planning Rubric

	Exceptional 3	Advanced 2	Basic 1	Inadequate 0
Assumptions list	Provides an **exhaustive** list of assumptions that **reflects all parts of the plan**.	Provides a list of assumptions that **reflects most parts of the plan**.	Provides a **partial** list that evidences a basic analysis of the plan.	List is mostly **incomplete.**
Prioritization of assumptions	Prioritizes the assumptions **accurately** by evaluating the level of danger if the assumption proves wrong and the level of confidence that the assumption is true.	Prioritizes assumptions **mostly** correctly, although some choices are questionable.	Makes an effort to prioritize, but prioritization does not consider the level of danger if the assumption proves wrong and the level of confidence that the assumption is true.	Assumptions are **not prioritized**.
Plan to test and learn	Proposes a **simple, inexpensive plan** to test and learn to ensure that key assumptions prove true.	Proposes a plan to test and learn, **but a few aspects may be overly complicated or expensive**.	Proposes a plan to test and learn, but **many aspects are overly complicated and/or expensive**.	Proposes a plan, but it **does not focus on key assumptions OR** is incomplete.

Implementation Rubric

	Exceptional 3	Advanced 2	Basic 1	Inadequate 0
What must change?	Considers **all parts of the blended-learning plan** to develop a thorough understanding of the components of the operation that must change to deliver the new learning design.	Considers **most parts of the plan** to develop an understanding of the components of the operation that must change to deliver the new learning design.	Considers **only part of the plan**; the team does not have an understanding of the components of the operation that must change.	**Does not consider the plan** when deciding what must change in the current operation.

	Exceptional 3	Advanced 2	Basic 1	Inadequate 0
Milestones	Proposes a list of milestones for each year that meets all requirements. *Requirements:* • The list is comprehensive and organized. • The milestones are specific, reasonable, and sufficient to achieve the desired outcomes. • Milestones include discovery-driven planning checkpoints. • Includes both pilot and rollout phases, with extra detail provided for the pilot phase.	The list of milestones meets most requirements.	The list of milestones meets one or two requirements.	**Ignores** the work of identifying key milestones.
Pilot tests	The milestones include a **realistic** pilot test and a **sound** plan for implementing the necessary changes to establish the pilot.	Proposes a **mostly** realistic and sound pilot test plan.	Proposes a **partial** pilot test plan.	**Overlooks** the pilot-testing phase.

Template for blended-learning plan

To work on your plan as a Google Doc, go to bit.ly/BlendedPlanTemplate and click on the "Make a copy" icon. A new page will open with your own copy of the template here.

Cover page

State the name of your blended-learning initiative and list key contact information for your organization and project manager.

Section 1: Rallying Cry

1. **Context.** Provide a few sentences of context about your district, charter management organization, or school (collectively referred to as "site"). This may include basic information like the site's location, size, and number of schools, as well as baseline data around academic, athletic, or other extracurricular successes and continued struggles. This context is important to provide outside readers with a basic overview of your setting.

2. **Problem(s).** State the top problem related to student achievement that you intend for student-centered learning to solve. Use baseline data to quantify the problem. If you are choosing more than one problem, such as one core problem and one nonconsumption

problem, name each initiative as Project 1, Project 2, and so forth for easy reference throughout the rest of your plan.

3. **SMART goals.** For the problem statement you have crafted, state your SMART goal. Be sure to provide metrics that show where you are now and where you are aiming to be each year.

Section 2: Team

1. Select your type of team

Indicate which type of team you plan to organize to achieve your SMART goal.

Team type: ______________________________

Explain why this team is the right fit:

____

____

____

____

____

____

____

____

____

____

____

2. Identify your team members and project manager

List each team member whom you will recruit to lead your blended-learning initiative, what her role is in the school community, and why this person is right for the team. Pay attention to what role each team member will play on your functional, lightweight, heavyweight, or autonomous team.

Name: ____

Role: ____

Why on the team?

____

____

____

Name: ________________________________

Role: ________________________________

Why on the team?

Name:

Role:

Why on the team?

Name:

Role:

Why on the team?

Name:

Role:

Why on the team?

Name:

Role:

Why on the team?

____

____

____

Name: ____

Role: ____

Why on the team?

____

____

____

Name: ____

Role: ____

Why on the team?

____

____

____

Now circle the team member who will be the project leader or manager. Describe why this person is an ideal fit:

____

____

____

Section 3: Student experience

Day in the life of a hypothetical student

____

____

____

Week in the life of a hypothetical student

Section 4: Teacher experience

Identify the motivators that your design seeks to amplify for teachers. Describe the strategies that you plan to use to amplify these motivators.

Section 5: Physical and virtual environment

1. Audit the schools of implementation for your program and provide a summary of the devices, Wi-Fi access, software licenses, and facilities that are already available.

2. Provide an analysis of the ways in which your physical and virtual environment is already sufficient to deliver your intended models, and the places where you have gaps.

3. Describe your priorities for improving the physical and virtual infrastructure and space for the schools of implementation.

Section 6: Choose the model

Name the blended-learning model or combination of models you plan to implement, and describe why you made that decision.

Section 7: Culture

1. List three to four recurring problems or tasks that are the most important for students, teachers, and/or administrators to resolve day by day during your program.
2. For each of the high-priority, recurring tasks or problems you listed, identify a process or routine that could work to resolve it successfully.
3. Describe how the team will promote this process or routine to deeply plant it into the culture across the system.

You may complete this section by using the table here.

Recurring problem or task	Possible process or routine for resolving it	How team will promote the culture

Section 8: Budgets

Costs

School-Level Costs									
One-Time Expenses									
Cost Item	**Per-Unit Cost ($)**	**No. of Units**	**Subtotal ($)**	**Year 1**	**Year 2**	**Year 3**	**Year 4**	**Year 5**	**Notes**
Example: Chromebooks	250	10	2,500	2,500					
Total School-Level One-Time Expenses									
Recurring Expenses									
Cost Item	**Per-Unit Cost ($)**	**No. of Units**	**Subtotal ($)**	**Year 1**	**Year 2**	**Year 3**	**Year 4**	**Year 5**	**Notes**
Example: Chromebook refresh	250	3	750	—	—	750	750	750	
Total School-Level Recurring Expenses									

Central Costs									
One-Time Expenses									
Cost Item	**Per-Unit Cost ($)**	**No. of Units**	**Sub-total ($)**	**Year 1**	**Year 2**	**Year 3**	**Year 4**	**Year 5**	**Notes**
Example: District PD/ conference	50,000	1	50,000	50,000					
Total Central One-Time Expenses									
Recurring Expenses									
Cost Item	**Per-Unit Cost ($)**	**No. of Units**	**Sub-total ($)**	**Year 1**	**Year 2**	**Year 3**	**Year 4**	**Year 5**	**Notes**
Example: LMS license	10	2,500	25,000	12,500	25,000	25,000	25,000	25,000	We roll this out to only half of district in Year 1; therefore, we don't incur full cost until Year 2.

Central Costs									
One-Time Expenses									
Total Central Recurring Expenses									

Total School-Level and Central Costs						
	Year 1	**Year 2**	**Year 3**	**Year 4**	**Year 5**	**Total**
TOTAL Expenses (One-Time and Recurring)						

Revenue and savings

Funding							
Incremental Funding							
Item	**Year 1**	**Year 2**	**Year 3**	**Year 4**	**Year 5**	**Total**	**Notes**
Example: Philanthropic grant	20,000	20,000	20,000			60,000	
Total Incremental Funding							

Recurring Revenue and Savings							
Item	**Year 1**	**Year 2**	**Year 3**	**Year 4**	**Year 5**	**Total**	**Notes**
Example: Printing savings	150	300	500	500	500	1,950	There is a ramp-up until we realize full savings
Total Reallocation of Funds							

	Year 1	Year 2	Year 3	Year 4	Year 5	Total	Notes
TOTAL Funds Available							

Full budget

	Year 1	Year 2	Year 3	Year 4	Year 5	Total
TOTAL Funds Available						
TOTAL Expenses						
TOTAL Surplus (Deficit)						

Budget narrative

Section 9: Discovery-driven planning

Assumption	Risk (1, 2, 3)	Confidence (1, 2, 3)	Rank (Avg.)	Test

Section 10: Implementation

1. Refer to your SMART goal and the new student and teacher experiences you designed to achieve the goal. What components of your operations must change in order for you to implement this new design, and how must they change?

You may complete this section by using the Implementation Table here.

Component	What must change?	How must it change?
Example: Student experience (Schedules, curriculum, mentoring, tutoring, apprenticeships, wellness, access to data, etc.)	*Example:* Schedule for P.E.	*Example:* Increase length of P.E. blocks to increase physical exercise time

2. Using the Gantt Chart Template that follows or another project-management system, provide a timeline that shows your key milestones over the next three years, including discovery-driven planning checkpoints. The timeline should show both a pilot and rollout phase, with significant detail provided for the pilot phase.

Gantt Chart Template

ID	Task	No. of quarters to complete	Year 1				Year 2				Year 3			
			Q1	Q2	Q3	Q4	Q1	Q2	Q3	Q4	Q1	Q2	Q3	Q4
Example	Expand P.E. schedule	2		→	→	*Milestone: Expanded P.E. schedules in place for all middle school students at Alpha campus.								
1														
2														
3														
4														
5														

6														
7														
8														
9														
10														
11														
12														

Next steps

Many teams find that they gain valuable insights about how to improve their plan by subjecting it to peer review. Consider sharing your full draft with other teams and asking for their feedback. Provide them with the rubrics from this workbook to align their scoring to the theories and practices that have guided your planning. Review the feedback you receive and use it to inform your final draft.

With the final draft complete, you have the vision, design, and implementation steps to improve your school with blended learning. Move forward with confidence to transform teaching and learning for your students.

Index